I0605693

THE HOUSES OF
GUINNESS

THE HOUSES OF
GUINNESS

The Lives, Homes and Fortunes of the
Great Brewing Dynasty

ADRIAN TINNISWOOD

SCALA

First published in 2025 by
Scala Arts & Heritage Publishers Ltd
43 Great Ormond Street
London WC1N 3HZ, UK
www.scalapublishers.com
An imprint of B. T. Batsford Holdings Ltd.

ISBN 978-1-78551-607-8

Edited by Rachel Giles
Editorial team at Scala: Claire Young and Oliver Craske
Designed by James Alexander
Cover and case design by Eoghan O'Brien, Sanya Jain and James Alexander
Picture research by Maria Ranauro
Printed in Turkey

Scala is represented in UK and Europe by Abrams & Chronicle Books, 1 West Smithfield, London, EC1A 9JU and 57 rue Gaston Tessier, 75166 Paris, France.

Front cover: Kenwood on Hampstead Heath, saved and given to the British nation by Edward Cecil Guinness, Earl of Iveagh.

Back cover: The brothers Rupert, Ernest and Walter Guinness outside Farmleigh, probably in the late 1890s.

Page 1: An 18th-century stone temple that Oonagh Guinness rebuilt on her estate at Luggala, on the shores of Lough Tay, high in the Wicklow Hills.

Page 2: House party in September or October 1880 at Ashford Castle, which was transformed by Sir Arthur and Olive Guinness, Lord and Lady Ardilaun.

Pages 4–5: Autumn light at Luttrellstown Castle, once home of Aileen Guinness.

Page 8: Summer roses at Kelvedon Hall, bought and refurbished by Lady Honor Guinness and 'Chips' Channon.

About the Author

Adrian Tinniswood, OBE FSA, is a true chronicler of the country houses of the UK and Ireland, having published nineteen books on social and architectural history, including *The Long Weekend: Life in the English Country House Between the Wars*, a *New York Times* and *Sunday Times* bestseller, and *The Verneys: a True Story of Love, War and Madness in Seventeenth-Century England*, which was shortlisted for the BBC/Samuel Johnson Prize. He is Professor of British Cultural History at the University of Buckingham and Adjunct Professor of History at Maynooth University. He lives in the west of Ireland with his wife Helen and their cat.

Contents

Foreword

The Houses of Guinness beautifully captures the family's varied tastes in architecture and their lifestyles, with many wonderful vignettes along the way. It features glorious pictures and the essential character of the Guinness family spirit prevails. On reading this publication I was left far better informed of my family history, and I recommend it to social historians, aesthetes and architectural connoisseurs, and as a really enjoyable account for the casual reader.

It is a compelling tale, told property by property. These Guinnesses were a spirited lot, who built structures of considerable stature, and some would argue of much merit, the fate of which has been as colourful as the lives of my forebears who commissioned or bought and lived in them.

I commend Adrian's work here. It is an entertaining masterpiece on a subject which truly rewards.

Arthur Edward Guinness, 4th Lord Iveagh
Elveden, August 2025

Opposite
Helen's Tower at Clandeboye House.

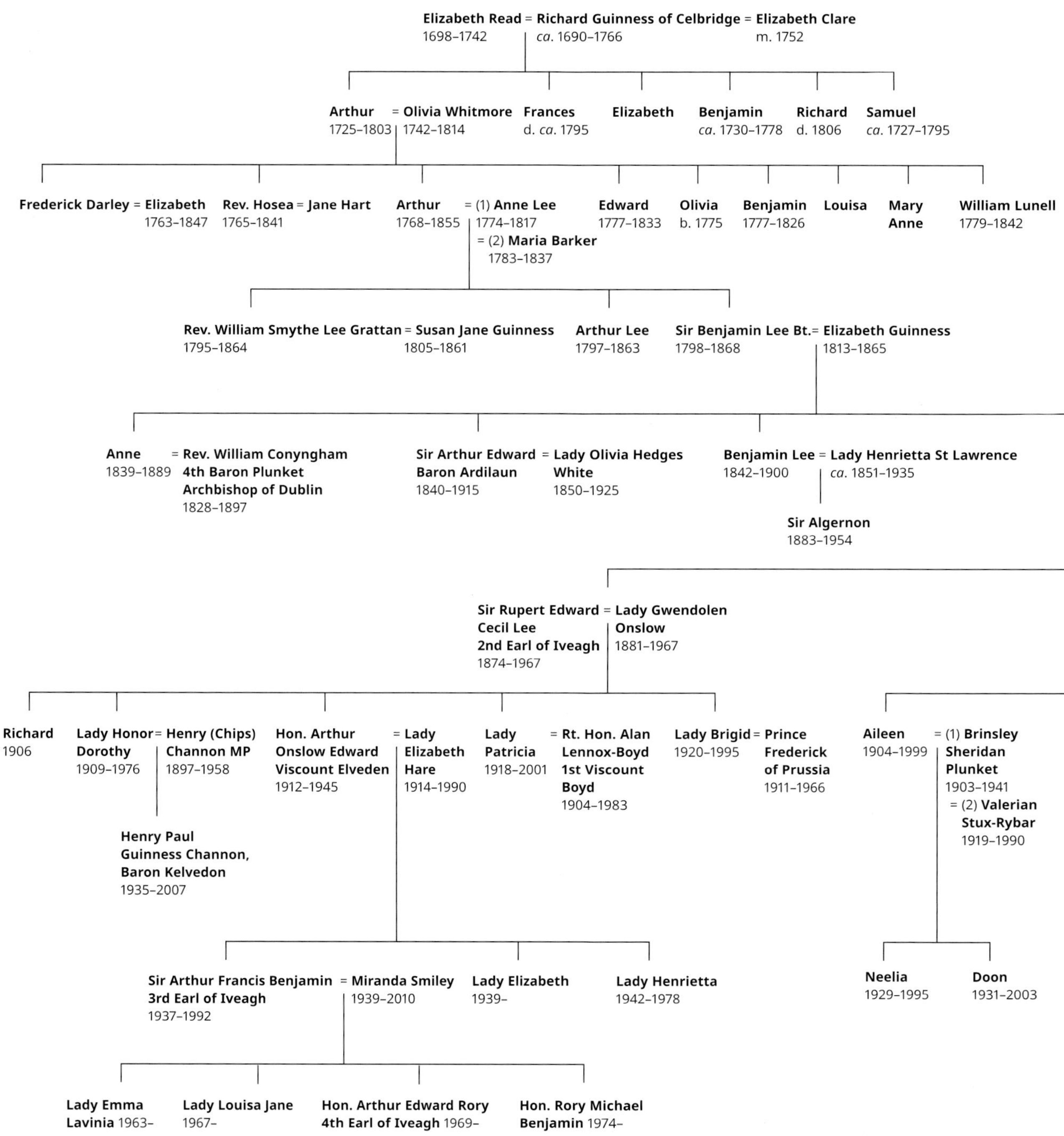
Elizabeth Read = Richard Guinness of Celbridge = Elizabeth Clare
1698–1742 ca. 1690–1766 m. 1752
Arthur = Olivia Whitmore
1725–1803 1742–1814
Frances
d. ca. 1795
Elizabeth
Benjamin
ca. 1730–1778
Richard
d. 1806
Samuel
ca. 1727–1795
Frederick Darley = Elizabeth
1763–1847
Rev. Hosea = Jane Hart
1765–1841
Arthur = (1) Anne Lee
1768–1855 1774–1817
= (2) Maria Barker
1783–1837
Edward
1777–1833
Olivia
b. 1775
Benjamin
1777–1826
Louisa
Mary Anne
William Lunell
1779–1842
Rev. William Smythe Lee Grattan = Susan Jane Guinness
1795–1864 1805–1861
Arthur Lee
1797–1863
Sir Benjamin Lee Bt. = Elizabeth Guinness
1798–1868 1813–1865
Anne = Rev. William Conyngham
1839–1889 4th Baron Plunket
Archbishop of Dublin
1828–1897
Sir Arthur Edward = Lady Olivia Hedges
Baron Ardilaun White
1840–1915 1850–1925
Benjamin Lee = Lady Henrietta St Lawrence
1842–1900 ca. 1851–1935
Sir Algernon
1883–1954
Sir Rupert Edward = Lady Gwendolen
Cecil Lee Onslow
2nd Earl of Iveagh 1881–1967
1874–1967
Richard
1906
Lady Honor = Henry (Chips)
Dorothy Channon MP
1909–1976 1897–1958
Henry Paul
Guinness Channon,
Baron Kelvedon
1935–2007
Hon. Arthur = Lady
Onslow Edward Elizabeth
Viscount Elveden Hare
1912–1945 1914–1990
Lady = Rt. Hon. Alan
Patricia Lennox-Boyd
1918–2001 1st Viscount
Boyd
1904–1983
Lady Brigid = Prince
1920–1995 Frederick
of Prussia
1911–1966
Aileen = (1) Brinsley
1904–1999 Sheridan
Plunket
1903–1941
= (2) Valerian
Stux-Rybar
1919–1990
Sir Arthur Francis Benjamin = Miranda Smiley
3rd Earl of Iveagh 1939–2010
1937–1992
Lady Elizabeth
1939–
Lady Henrietta
1942–1978
Neelia
1929–1995
Doon
1931–2003
Lady Emma
Lavinia 1963–
Lady Louisa Jane
1967–
Hon. Arthur Edward Rory
4th Earl of Iveagh 1969–
Hon. Rory Michael
Benjamin 1974–

A Guinness Family Tree

Dates given where known.

Key
b. born
m. married
d. died
Bt. baronet
ca. circa

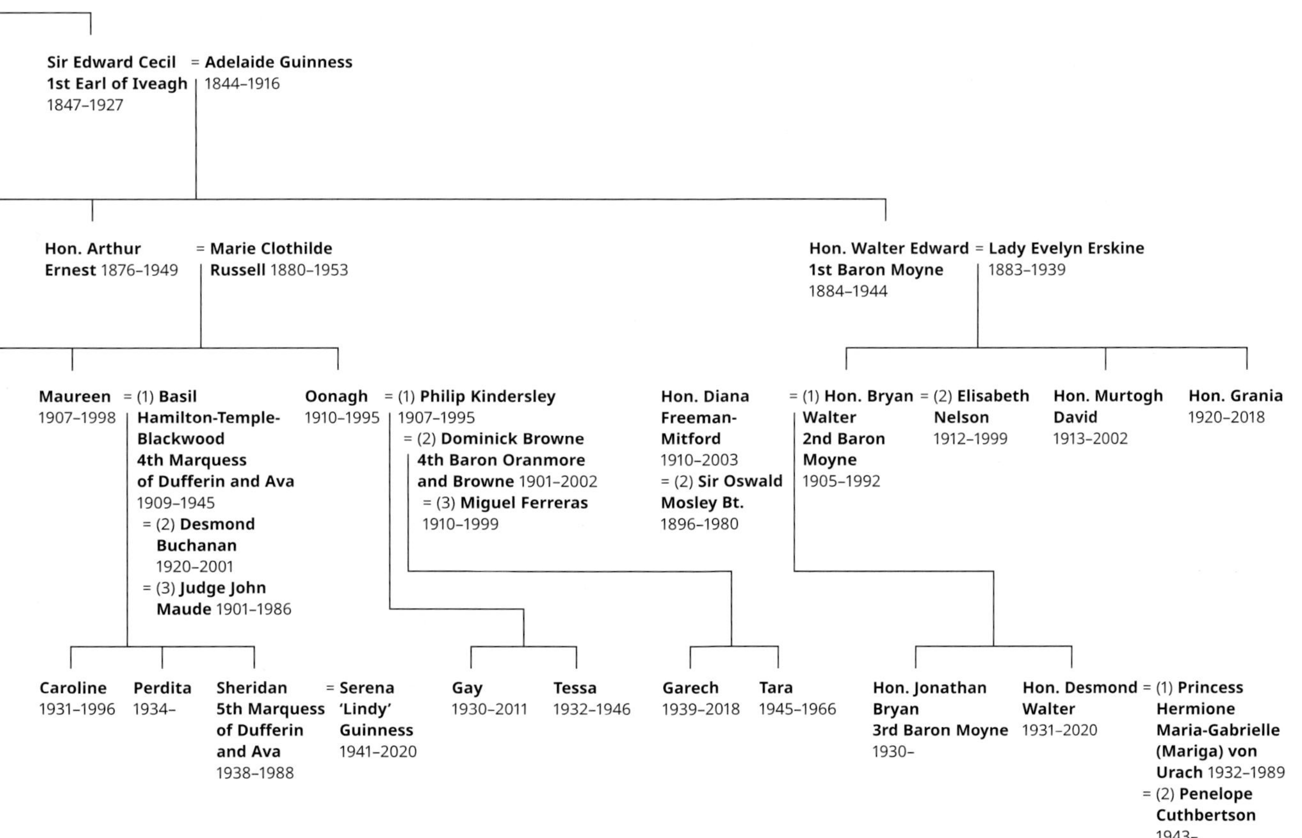

Introduction

As the old advertising slogan goes, 'Guinness is good for you.'

It has certainly been good for the Irish economy. From the day at the end of December 1759 when the thirty-four-year-old Arthur Guinness signed a lease on a run-down brewery on James's Street in Dublin, the firm has grown, until today Guinness is the biggest exporter of stout in the world, and somewhere in the region of 1.8 *billion* pints are drunk every year. There are Guinness breweries in forty-nine countries, although Arthur's James's Street complex is still the largest producer of what James Joyce in *Ulysses* so memorably called 'the foaming ebon ale'.

It has been good for the Guinness family, too. Although their direct connection with the firm that bears their name finally came to an end in 1997 when Guinness plc merged with Grand Metropolitan to form the beverage giant Diageo, for well over 200 years Arthur and his descendants prospered. Politically conservative Church of Ireland Protestants with a strong evangelical streak and an equally strong work ethic (most of them, anyway), they turned stout to liquid gold. When Benjamin Lee Guinness, who ran the business in the mid-nineteenth century, died in 1868 he was Ireland's first millionaire. Eighteen years later his son, Edward Cecil Guinness, floated the company on the Stock Exchange, while retaining one-third of the stock himself. When *he* died, in 1927, he was an earl and he left an estate valued at £11 million.

As their fortunes prospered, their ambitions grew, helped along by a strong sense of civic pride and social justice. It was a Guinness who restored Dublin's St Patrick's Cathedral. It was a Guinness who gave the 22-acre St Stephen's Green to the city, a Guinness who built hospitals and replaced slums with decent worker housing in Dublin and London, and donated Kenwood House to the public and filled it with fabulous works of art.

And like any *nouveaux riches* industrialists seeking to move up the social ladder, they bought, built, or remodelled rural retreats where they could entertain their friends, impress their business acquaintances and enjoy their wealth. These castles and country houses range from the modest Beaumont, a small Georgian villa in fields north of Dublin which was home to Arthur, his wife Olive and their ten children, to Farmleigh and Elveden Hall and the sadly demolished St Anne's, monumental

Above
A mid-20th century aerial view showing the full extent of the Guinness brewery at St James's Gate, Dublin, looking north-west towards the River Liffey.

examples of late-Victorian opulence, mansions which were fit to receive royalty – and which often did. Later generations might opt for a quieter elegance with exquisite and quintessentially English houses like Biddesden and Kelvedon, or throw caution and their fortunes to the wind with parties that seemed never to end, as Oonagh Guinness and her sister Aileen did at Luggala and Luttrellstown.

But old or new, extravagant or sedate, the houses of Guinness are a testament to the wealth of a single family. More than that: they offer a unique glimpse into a privileged way of life that flourished in the nineteenth and twentieth centuries and then passed away. They have stories to tell about love and loss, about saints and sinners. Their walls remember tales of failure as well as success, bearing witness to lives well lived and opportunities squandered. And the ghosts of the men and women who made them still walk through their marble halls and great glass palm houses and magnificent ballrooms.

This is their story, too.

Adrian Tinnsiwood, Summer 2025

1

BEAUMONT HOUSE

Dublin

The sick, the worried and the well who navigate their way through the sprawling campus of Dublin's Beaumont Hospital rarely notice the Georgian villa that stands at the heart of the complex, looking oddly out of place among the sleek modern clinics and the overflowing car parks. And if they do, fewer still realise as they stroll past that they are seeing a landmark in Irish and British history, a building where a dynasty was born. Because 250 years ago this little villa was the home of Arthur Guinness.

Arthur was the founder of the Guinness family's fortunes. Born in 1725, he was the eldest son of Richard Guinness, the steward and agent of Dr Arthur Price, a fiercely ambitious rector of Celbridge in County Kildare, who acquired one bishopric after another until by the 1740s he was Archbishop of Cashel and Vice-Chancellor of Trinity College Dublin. Tradition has it that Arthur was named after Price, who was his godfather and who left him £100 when he died in 1752.

Opposite
The house and grounds at Beaumont, in a Guinness family painting, artist and date unknown.

Right
Beaumont House today, in the grounds of Beaumont Hospital.

Arthur started brewing beer in a small way in Leixlip, County Kildare, in 1755. At this stage he was brewing ale rather than the dark porter which was to make his name. Four years later he began to negotiate a lease on a disused brewery at St James's Gate in Dublin, a four-acre site which consisted of a house, a brew house, two malt houses, outhouses and stables. He acquired the brewery and the house that went with it for 9,000 years at a modest annual rent of £45, and quickly began to engage in the civic life of Dublin, while competing with the other hundred or more breweries operating in the city.

In 1761 Arthur married Olivia (Olive) Whitmore, the well-connected 19-year-old daughter of a Dublin grocer and his wife, Mary Grattan. He was 36. And three years later, armed with a useful contribution from his deceased father-in-law in the shape of a £1,000 dowry, he bought – or just possibly built – Beaumont, an elegant if unambitious villa a mile or so north of the Guinness brewery at St James's Gate.

Beaumont's origins are something of a mystery. Jean Rocque's highly detailed 1757 map of Dublin County shows a field where the house should be. If Rocque's map is correct, then either Beaumont was built and then sold to the Guinnesses within the space of seven years or, less

Below
Family portraits of the first Arthur Guinness and his wife Olivia Whitmore.

Above
North-western sheet of Jean Rocque's map of the city and suburbs of Dublin. The site of Beaumont is highlighted in red.

likely, actually built by Arthur. It was (and still is) a pleasant two-storey house of five bays, with slightly later neoclassical Adamesque interiors commissioned by Arthur and Olive at some point. With views south across Dublin city to the Wicklow Mountains, and on a clear day, to the north and the Mourne Mountains, it was a substantial house, although scarcely substantial enough to hold the twenty-one children that Olive bore Arthur over the next thirty years. (Only ten survived into adulthood.) But it was a country house, and a country house was an essential adjunct for a man of ambition.

Arthur divided his time between Beaumont and the house at St James's Gate. In the 1770s he made what would turn out to be the most momentous decision of his life, opting to concentrate on making porter and, eventually, to give up producing ale completely. There is an entry in the firm's record books, dated 1 April 1799: 'Today ... was brewed the last ale brew.'[1] The business prospered, and by the early nineteenth century Guinness's was the leading brewer in Dublin.

Left
Exterior of 1 Thomas Street, Arthur and Olivia Guinness's home that was included with the original 1759 lease of the St James's Gate brewery. Photographed *ca.*1906–10.

Below
Interior of 1 Thomas Street, 1948. The bust is of Arthur's grandson, Benjamin Lee Guinness. The bomb is a replica of the one that struck the Guinness ship *SS Carrowdore* off Dublin in 1941 and incorporates the original tail and fins. (No one was injured.)

Arthur Guinness died in 1803, leaving Beaumont to his eldest son Hosea, who after Winchester and Oxford had gone into the Church and thus was 'not being in any line of life whereby he is likely by industry to enlarge his property', as Arthur said rather pointedly in his will.[2] Effective control of his businesses (which now included flour mills) passed to his second son, Arthur, who had been made a full partner in the business in 1798; thus establishing a pattern that would last for three generations of handing the brewery over, not to the eldest boy, but to the son judged best to manage it.

And Arthur, who is usually referred to as Arthur II to distinguish him from his father, managed it very well indeed, sending the Guinness porter all over Ireland and exporting to England, which became an increasingly important market. Sales rose from 6,704 hogsheads at the beginning of the century to 65,541 hogsheads in 1850. That's over 3.5 million gallons. At the same time, Arthur II

Right
Family portrait of Arthur Guinness II.

Overleaf
The Cooperage Yard at St James's Gate. Throughout the 19th century the Guinness brewery expanded and became ever busier. In the 1870s a narrow-gauge railway was built to transport raw materials around the site and casks of beer to the river for onward shipping.

became involved in banking, and followed his father by taking an active role in the civic life of the city. He was Governor of the Bank of Ireland, receiving George IV during the king's inspection of the Bank as part of his visit to Ireland in 1821; and for many years he was President of the Dublin Chamber of Commerce. His faith was Protestant, and his politics were conservative, but by no means reactionary: he supported Catholic emancipation, and spoke in support of parliamentary reform, declaring that 'a great change was taking place all over the world... Everywhere the grand principle was beginning to be asserted that Governments were instituted only for the benefit of the people.'[3] For years he was a friend and supporter of Daniel O'Connell, 'the Liberator', only parting company with him over the repeal of the Union, which Arthur II thought was a step too far.

C S W R

A devout evangelical, he nevertheless knew that sometimes faith without works won't do the trick; and he donated to a bewildering range of good causes, most of them connected to Protestantism. He gave £10 towards an organ for the Free Church in Great Charles Street, Dublin (originally a Methodist chapel, but by the time that Arthur II made his donation, it belonged to the Church of Ireland); £25 to Dublin's Protestant Orphanage and £40 to the Dublin and Kildare Clergy Widows' Fund.

At some point in the early nineteenth century Hosea Guinness sold Beaumont House to Arthur II, who lived there for the rest of his life with his extended family. Married twice, to Anne Lee who died in 1817 and then to Maria Barker who died in 1837, altogether he fathered nine children. The early Guinnesses were nothing if not prolific. Several unmarried daughters lived with him at Beaumont. Then there were brothers, spinster sisters, around forty nephews and nieces, widowed cousins, distant relations, all of whom operated within an accepted kinship network which allowed them, not exactly to sponge off the de facto head of the family, but certainly to accept his hospitality at frequent intervals. And through it all Arthur II remained, in the words of one of his many relatives, a 'perfect specimen of a Christian gentleman ... determined his should be regarded as a Christian household.'[4] After dinner his many guests were expected to listen to a sermon given by the local minister, followed by prayers, before they could depart. The clergyman who preached at his funeral declared that 'The Bible was his constant companion in his study and I rarely entered it and met him there that the book was not open; and invariably, when alone, he would conclude the interview by saying, "Let us pray."'[5]

In spite of its proximity to Dublin, Beaumont was a country estate, actively farmed by Arthur II. Even today, the villa is sometimes dismissed as a 'farmhouse', although to contemporaries it was 'a noble mansion [that] has about it a look of highest gentility'.[6] Arthur II kept sheep – at least, he tried to keep sheep. In the summer of 1818, a snippet in one of the local newspapers recorded that one of the Beaumont sheep had been killed and butchered one night: the peace officer was in hot pursuit of the offenders, although history does not record if they were ever apprehended. By the 1850s Arthur II also had a dairy herd. His steward, a competent man named Gillespie, proudly informed the *Farmer's Gazette* of an experiment made at Beaumont in which 16.5 pints of milk taken from one of Arthur's cows had yielded an impressive 28 ounces of butter. He put this down to diet: at Beaumont, the dairy cows were given 'a large supply of mangel-wurzel, with plenty of good, sweet hay'.[7]

Gillespie also oversaw traditional harvest home celebrations at Beaumont, with help from Arthur's gardener, Mr McLean (who was admitted to the Royal Horticultural Society of Ireland in 1853, after winning prizes and plaudits for everything from his calceolarias to his cucumbers). In September 1851, for example, one of the coach-houses was fitted up and decorated with evergreens and flowers. The walls were hung with an assortment of fruit and vegetables – turnips, carrots, grapes and some of those mangel-wurzels – and Gillespie's chair was flanked by two long spades, carrying in large letters the somewhat cryptic mottos 'Success to spade labour' and 'The true fertilizer'. Around fifty men and boys sat down at two tables, one presided over by Gillespie, the other by McLean, to a dinner of beef, mutton, ham and plum pudding, after which Arthur put in an appearance to propose a toast to the Queen and Prince Albert, at which the ladies who had joined the party broke into the national anthem, the tables were cleared and there was dancing. It would be nice to think that Arthur II joined in, although by this time he was 83 and, as he wrote to his son Benjamin Lee Guinness, 'patiently abiding His time for calling me to that Place of Everlasting Rest.'[8] So perhaps not.

Arthur II died at Beaumont on 9 June 1855, 'venerated by all who knew him'.[9] He was 87, and Benjamin Lee Guinness had been in effective charge of the brewery for decades, ably assisted by master brewer John Purser and hindered rather than helped by Benjamin Lee's elder brother, Arthur Lee Guinness. But Arthur II was still a man of substance in Dublin society, and although he wanted a private funeral, his wishes were ignored. The cortege left Beaumont for the family plot at Mount Jerome, on the other side of the city, at nine on the morning of 14 June, led by a hearse drawn by six horses, with mutes bearing wands and wearing mourning badges. Then came the private family coaches; then coachloads of servants; then the Lord Mayor of Dublin, Sir Edward McDonnell, in his state carriage, and then a long, long line of coaches, nearly a hundred in all. There were judges and lawyers, businessmen and town councillors. As the cortege wound its way through Dublin, more coaches joined, and groups of people stood with their heads bowed on the street. By the time it reached Mount Jerome an enormous crowd had gathered to pay its respects.

The family sold Beaumont House soon afterwards.

2

ST ANNE'S

Dublin

There is a rough sketch of St Anne's in the Irish Architecture Archive in Dublin. Made in about 1837, it does not suggest that this, one of the grandest of all the Guinness mansions, was a thing of beauty.

Drawn by the Cork architect Henry Hill, the sketch shows a big, muddled house with pediments and oriel windows, battlements and gables and classical columns, all dominated by a tall observation tower on the roof. Projecting a full thirty-six feet above the roofline, this belvedere was based on the first-century BC Gallo-Roman Mausoleum of Glanum in Saint-Rémy-de-Provence, and placed to make the most of some spectacular views out across Dublin Bay – without, it has to be said, much regard for architectural coherence.

Known in the mid-nineteenth century as St Ann's without the 'e', and before that as Thornhill, St Anne's, on the northern outskirts of Dublin, was the Guinness family's first substantial country house, much larger than Beaumont. But it wasn't substantial enough. Soon after Arthur II's two sons, Benjamin Lee Guinness and Arthur Lee Guinness,

Opposite
Clock tower built by Benjamin Lee Guinness in 1850 on the St Anne's estate. It is one of the follies still standing today in St Anne's Park, Dublin.

Right
Sketch of St Anne's by Henry Hill, *ca.*1837.

Left
Portrait of Benjamin Lee Guinness by Stephen Catterson Smith.

jointly bought the house and its fifty-acre estate in 1835, they set about extending both, a move that was prompted by Benjamin Lee's marriage in February 1837 to a cousin, Elizabeth Guinness; and, perhaps, by their father's retirement from the family business two years later. Although we don't know much about Thornhill before the Guinnesses, Henry Hill's sketch almost certainly represents a remodelling carried out around this time. A cousin, Frederick Darley Ogilby, who arrived from America in 1840 to visit his Guinness relations, remarked on the house's 'castle-like appearance, being of irregular Gothic construction with a high tower rising from the centre'. He was impressed by the view, by the gardens, and by 'the greatest profusion of the costliest furniture'.[1]

He was also impressed by Arthur Lee Guinness, who in spite of being joint owner of St Anne's (and of the brewery), didn't spend much time there, preferring instead to live in his own house at St James's Gate. Arthur Lee was an aesthete before aesthetes were invented. His drawing room, recalled Frederick, was furnished 'in Chinese style and most richly'. The house was crowded with statues, paintings and stuffed birds. There was a fountain in the yard, and among a scattering of gods and goddesses, there was 'a little figure of ambiguous character'.[2]

Arthur Lee was also a figure of ambiguous character. Around the time of Frederick's visit, he was involved in an affair with a brewery clerk, Dion Boucicault, who was paid – either by Arthur Lee or by his father – to decamp to London, where he made a name for himself as an actor and a writer of melodramas. Perhaps as a result of this affair, Arthur Lee withdrew from the brewery partnership, in return for a payment of £12,000 and some shares. He also gave up his share in St Anne's, left his little house at the brewery with its chinoiserie and its gods and goddesses, and bought Stillorgan House, an early eighteenth-century mansion south of Dublin, where he spent his time composing pantheistic poetry and getting into more scrapes, until his exasperated father urged him to show 'some token of his being awakened to a sense of the value of the Gospel of our Lord Jesus Christ'.[3] He left Stillorgan in 1860 for a smaller house down in Wicklow, where he died three years later.

Meanwhile, Benjamin Lee and his wife Elizabeth were establishing themselves as one of Dublin society's leading couples, while the brewery went from strength to strength, until by the 1860s it was the largest porter brewery in the world, and Benjamin Lee was a very rich man indeed – Ireland's first millionaire, in fact. He was politically active, becoming Lord Mayor of Dublin in 1851, and sitting as Conservative MP for Dublin from 1865 until his death three years later. And he consolidated the Guinness family's reputation for philanthropic works, donating to various charities and working tirelessly to restore St Patrick's Cathedral in the city (see pp. 76–80).

In 1852 Benjamin Lee bought Ashford, a shooting lodge on the shore of Lough Corrib in County Mayo which had belonged to the Oranmore and Browne family for centuries; and in 1856, a year after his father died, he decided he needed a more prestigious address in Dublin, and bought 80 St Stephen's Green, a fine town house built in 1736–7 to the designs of one of Ireland's greatest architects, Richard Castle. (He also had a house in London's fashionable Mayfair.) Both Ashford and 80 St

Above
Statues and topiary in the gardens at St Anne's.

Stephen's Green would figure largely in the lives of future generations of Guinnesses. So would the Oranmore and Browne family, come to that.

But St Anne's remained Benjamin Lee's principal residence, and this was where he and Elizabeth raised their children – a mere four, this time, Anne, Arthur, Benjamin and Edward. (One of Benjamin Lee's first works at St Anne's was a sham ruin which he put up over the entrance drive to commemorate Anne's birth in 1839.) Benjamin Lee and Elizabeth added an orangery to the house and laid out new gardens peppered with yew topiary and classical statues brought back by Benjamin Lee from his travels in Italy. They built a little 'Pompeian' temple beside an artificial lake below the house. In fact, their new gardens seem to have been quite full of incident: golden pheasants strutted around in an aviary; there was an hermitage, several grottoes, a 'Druidic circle' of basaltic rocks taken from the famous Giants' Causeway in County Antrim; a replica of a Herculanean villa, complete with a bronze of a Roman soldier in the centre of its courtyard; and two great terraces which made the most of the spectacular views across Dublin Bay.

But when it came to the house itself, it was Benjamin Lee's eldest son, Arthur, who turned St Anne's into a palace fit for a prince. On his father's death in 1868 Arthur inherited a baronetcy. Now Sir Arthur, he also inherited Ashford, the shooting lodge in Galway which is the subject of the

Right
Sir Arthur (later Lord Ardilaun) and his wife Lady Olive Guinness with her mother, the Countess of Bantry (right), 1877.

next chapter; and St Anne's. Socially ambitious, Sir Arthur married into the Irish peerage in 1871 – his bride was Lady Olivia (Olive) Hedges-White, daughter of the 3rd Earl of Bantry – and five years later he gave up his interest in the brewery in return for a very hefty £600,000, leaving his younger brother Edward in charge. A third brother, named Benjamin Lee after their father, went into the army and played no part in the business. Anne, their sister, had married an impeccably Protestant aristocrat: her husband was William Conyngham Plunket, 4th Baron Plunket, Dean of Christ Church Cathedral and Archbishop of Dublin.

Sir Arthur continued the philanthropic family tradition begun by his father, pouring his fortune into good works, the best known of which was his purchase of the 22-acre St Stephen's Green in Dublin, which he presented to the nation for the use of all its citizens. After years of work landscaping the park, it was opened on 27 July 1880, three months after Sir Arthur was raised to the peerage as Baron Ardilaun of Ashford, taking his title from the Irish *Ard Oileáin*, the 'high island' in Lough Corrib. He had, said *John Bull* at the time, 'shown in the management of riches a well-directed munificence that is somewhat rare'.[4] Shelters and a superintendent's cottage in the park were designed by the eccentric Kerry architect James Franklin Fuller, who was the architect to St Patrick's Cathedral, and who had worked for Benjamin Lee Guinness on the latter's town house, 80 St Stephen's Green, in the early 1860s. Fuller had a thriving country house practice. Unfortunately, he also had a habit of falling out with his aristocratic clients, perhaps because of his unorthodox approach to his accounts (he didn't keep any) and his correspondence (he didn't answer any).

In about 1873 Lord Ardilaun, as I'll call him from now on, employed Fuller to remodel St Anne's, vastly extending it in the process. It was an ambitious scheme, turning St Anne's into a huge Italianate mansion and introducing that much-needed element of architectural coherence. And it took seven years to complete. But architect and client parted company on bad terms before the work was finished. We don't know exactly what the trouble was, and Fuller continued to work for Ardilaun's brother Edward well into the 1880s; Fuller himself hinted that he was not prepared to exhibit the kind of social servility that Ardilaun expected from those he employed. The architect's 1916 autobiography, *Omniana*, in which he cheerfully described his rather carefree way with his clients' accounts, contains a damning passage about an unnamed multi-millionaire, famous for his philanthropy, who had been made a lord, a plutocrat turned autocrat turned aristocrat. 'I could not bring myself to appraise him at his own valuation,' wrote Fuller cryptically. 'We rubbed along for three or four years ... and then we drifted apart.'[5]

Whatever the cause of the rift, Ardilaun turned to another architect, George Coppinger Ashlin, to complete St Anne's. Ashlin, a Gothicist who had worked with A.W.N. Pugin's son, Edward Welby Pugin, was primarily a church architect: his entry in the *Dictionary of Irish Biography* notes that he worked on at least sixty churches and cathedrals in Ireland, as well as public buildings including a lunatic asylum at Portrane in County Dublin which at a cost of £300,000 was then the most expensive secular building ever seen in Ireland. At St Anne's, Ashlin was content to follow Fuller's florid Italianate scheme, which was after all well underway by the time he arrived on the scene.

By the time the remodelling was completed in 1880, the mansion was massive, twice the size of Ardilaun's father Benjamin Lee's house, and opulent in the extreme. It was also a good deal more coherent than the earlier building. A single-storey classical portico beneath a pediment led into a huge galleried entrance hall lined with marble columns, which in turn led to a faintly Renaissance-looking marble staircase. A prominent

Below
The architects employed by Lord Ardilaun to turn St Anne's into a palace: James Franklin Fuller (left), who began it and fell out with his patron, and George Coppinger Ashlin, who completed it.

Above
Exterior rear view of St Anne's showing the Palm Garden.

feature was an internal courtyard, 66 feet long by 38 feet wide and rising up the full height of the building. Described on plans as the 'Palm Garden', this court had a glass roof and in early photographs was filled with palm trees and other exotic plants.

In other ways, though, the layout of the mansion was typical of late-Victorian country house planning. The male domain, consisting of Lord Ardilaun's study, a billiard room and a smoking room, was situated on one side of the palm court, away from the main reception rooms, although in a slight departure from convention, the study was next to the front door and looked out on the entrance drive, so that Lord Ardilaun could see visitors approaching. (It was more usual for the butler to keep a lookout for visitors, so that he could appear at the door to greet them as if by magic.) The drawing room and the dining room ran along the south side and were placed to make the most of the views. In fact, the drawing room was built at a 60-degree angle to the garden front for that

Above
The galleried entrance hall of St Anne's.

reason. Olive Ardilaun's boudoir was on the first floor, and it opened onto a balcony which, again, gave views over the bay.

The domestic offices – kitchen, still room, servants' hall, and coach houses – were all on the north side of the house, presided over by the housekeeper's room and the butler's pantry and bedroom. The 36 ft-high tower on the roof was taken down and relocated to a less prominent position beside a lake in the grounds.

Like any wealthy aristocratic couple at the turn of the century, the Ardilauns led peripatetic lives. They were often in London, where Lord Ardilaun spoke occasionally in the House of Lords, usually on Irish matters, and whilst there they lived at 11 Carlton House Terrace, which was itself rather grand, with lots of marble and mirrors and gilding and French furniture. They also had a house on Leeson Street in Dublin; and two more country houses in Ireland which they rarely visited. Through her father, the 3rd Earl of Bantry, Olive Lady Ardilaun owned Macroom Castle

in County Cork, where she had spent some of her childhood; and in 1899 Lord Ardilaun bought Muckross Abbey in County Kilkenny for a reputed £60,000. The estate had belonged to his wife's uncle and seemed likely to be broken up when it came on the market: it was presumably Lady Ardilaun who persuaded her husband to keep it in the family.

Reminiscing about her life on one of her frequent charitable hospital visits, Olive Ardilaun once described to a ward full of astonished Dublin paupers how things were arranged when she went from St Anne's to her London house. The head coachman, Horton, would leave three or four days before her to sail over with a carriage, a groom and a pair of horses. Then the second coachman would drive her, her maid and a footman down to Dun Laoghaire, then known as Kingstown, where the Ardilauns' agent would meet her and take her and her maid aboard the waiting steam packet to the cabins engaged for them. These cabins were filled with flowers taken from her own garden at St Anne's. When they arrived into Holyhead, the footman would see them to their reserved carriage on the London train and magically appear at the carriage window whenever the train stopped at a station to make sure that she didn't need anything. When the train pulled into Euston, there would be Horton and Lady Ardilaun's own carriage waiting to carry her to Carlton House Terrace.

Both of the Ardilauns took their wealth and their responsibilities very seriously. But they still managed to enjoy life. At any one time they might be hosting a shooting party at Ashford, or presiding over various charitable committees in Dublin, or attending a state ball at Buckingham Palace, or wintering in the south of France. But St Anne's was home. 'A magnificent place furnished in sumptuous fashion,' gushed the *Tatler* in 1905, explaining that this was where Lady Ardilaun 'entertains regally in the season.'[6] Her visitors included actors and playwrights and senior judges. Countess Cadogan, wife of the Viceroy of Ireland, might come for lunch. Even the elderly Queen Victoria, on her last visit to Ireland in the spring of 1900, made a point of stopping briefly at St Anne's while out on an afternoon drive, so that Lady Ardilaun could present her with a bunch of primroses.

The couple usually took a party to the Dublin Horse Show, where Lord Ardilaun was president and praise for his wife's outfits filled the society pages. ('Lady Ardilaun ... was attired in a lovely gown of écru gauze elaborately trimmed with black lace and embroidery'.[7]) There were dinner parties and luncheon parties, and garden parties for various groups of Dublin dignitaries and, on one occasion at least, for shopworkers from

Opposite
The Annie Lee Tower Bridge in the grounds of St Anne's, built by Benjamin Lee Guinness to mark the birth of his daughter Anne Lee in 1838.

the clothing store of Forrest & Sons on Grafton Street, some of whom came on their bicycles to picnic under the trees, while others 'were conveyed by the more prosaic wagonette'.*

The Ardilauns had no children, and after Lord Ardilaun's death at the age of seventy-four in January 1915 his widow cut a lonely figure, rattling around in the vast mansion with only a dozen or so servants for company. According to Lady Gregory, who visited St Anne's several times to enlist Olive Ardilaun's support for the Abbey Theatre, 'her lovely garden is, she says, the one thing that keeps her there.'[8]

In 1916 Olive invited a cousin and goddaughter to come to St Anne's as her companion. Katherine Everett, whose artist husband had decamped to Paris before the war and left her with two boys to look after, and who was then working as a gardener-companion in the New Forest, jumped at the offer. And as her current employer pointed out when she bid her a reluctant farewell, 'one ought never to neglect really rich relations.'[9]

Katherine didn't have to live in. There were several good-sized villas nearby, a by-product of Lord Ardilaun's tendency to buy up neighbouring estates; and she was offered one of these, Sybil Hill, as a permanent home for her and her boys. It was just over a mile away from the mansion, giving Katherine a degree of independence and helping her and Olive to avoid the feeling that she was the paid help.

But she quickly found out that life with her cousin was not going to be all roses. Sybil Hill had a leaking roof, no electricity, a cracked boiler and three old-fashioned water closets that didn't work. When she mentioned this to Olive, the response was, 'Well, my dear, if you don't like it, you had better go back to England.'[10] Having sold her house in England and moved all her furniture over to Ireland, a stunned Katherine had little choice but to pay for improvements to Sybil Hill out of her own pocket. When they were done, however, Lady Ardilaun asked to see the accounts, and made out a cheque for £100 more than she had spent, saying calmly that the extra was for carpets and curtains. As Katherine wrote in her memoirs, she soon realised that Lady Ardilaun's initial response was a reflex reaction to having been very rich and surrounded

* *Dublin Evening Telegraph*, 16 July 1897, p. 2. This hospitality was in marked contrast to the situation at Macroom, where Lady Ardilaun caused a storm by refusing to open the Castle grounds, because the last time she had done so members of the public had damaged shrubs and flowers and assaulted the caretaker. She would never again allow the castle to be used for such purposes, she told the town council. It took a £200 cheque for the relief of the poor and sick of the district to make local people forgive that slight.

by sycophants and hustlers for most of her life. She had always been on her guard against attempts to take advantage of her money and her generosity.

If Katherine was unimpressed with Sybil Hill, she hated St Anne's. Although the remodelling was less than forty years old when she moved there, already it was beginning to look overblown and old-fashioned, like so much Victorian domestic architecture. The exterior had a certain grandeur, perhaps; but 'nothing can be said in favour of the interior,' she declared.[11] The glass roof over the palm garden leaked; the central heating didn't work; and the general effect, achieved by the Ardilauns'

Right
Olive, Lady Ardilaun, probably in the 1880s.

over-reliance on a firm of London decorators to furnish the house, was of an out-of-date luxury hotel. The great hall was too dark, the marble staircase was too cold, and as for the Ardilauns' taste in art:

> On the landing where the steps divided to ascend in two flights sat a female figure, also in cold white marble, hampered in her clearly expressed desire to appear modest by the lack of any rag of clothing.[12]

Katherine much preferred a town house, 42 St Stephen's Green, a few hundred yards away from 80 St Stephen's Green, the house bought by Olive's father-in-law and currently occupied by her brother-in-law Edward. Katherine had persuaded her cousin to use 42 in the winter instead of moving into the Shelbourne Hotel, her usual practice when she found the mausoleum-like St Anne's too cold for comfort. That was perhaps because Katherine was allowed to decorate the house herself, combing Dublin antique shops for suitable furniture.

St Anne's was untouched by the War of Independence and the civil war that followed, although Lady Ardilaun and Katherine Everett, who both supported Britain, knew British soldiers who died and deplored what they saw as atrocities perpetrated by the rebels. Katherine, who used to cycle the mile and a quarter from St Anne's to Sybil Hill every night, was sometimes stopped by armed men who emerged out of the darkness and warned her not to say anything if she saw lights or heard whistles in the darkness, or 'your place will go up'.[13] And she knew that her outbuildings were frequently used by fugitives on the run from the authorities.

When the two women heard that the Black and Tans had occupied Olive's old family home of Macroom Castle, Lady Ardilaun persuaded Katherine to travel the 200 miles across Ireland to Cork to arrange for furniture and paintings to be shipped back to St Anne's, a task she approached with energy and enthusiasm. And when news came in August 1922 that Macroom had been burned by anti-treatyites as they retreated before advancing Free State soldiers, and Lady Ardilaun was in despair and frantic for news of her home, Katherine set off again by train for Macroom. This time, though, she found the line was damaged and bridges down beyond Limerick, forcing her to cycle the final 60 miles alone through what was in effect a war zone. She didn't hesitate. When she eventually arrived, she found the Castle still smouldering. But the caretaker, an old woman named McCarthy, had demanded that the men carry out the furniture and Lady Ardilaun's things before they set it ablaze, and most of her belongings were saved to be sent back by sea from Cork to St Anne's.

Olive Ardilaun died unexpectedly at 42 St Stephen's Green on 13 December 1925. She was seventy-five, although the papers said she was seventy. St Anne's went to her nephew, Bishop Plunket, although in her will she pointed out that it was far too big and expensive to run. In fact, she urged Plunket to demolish it and build something smaller, 'or to reduce the existing house to the dimension of the original house as built by Sir Benjamin [Lee] Guinness'.[14] He did neither.

Olive left Katherine £5,000 and the paintings and furniture from Macroom, 'as it was she who went to Macroom and rescued them from the clutches of the Black and Tans when they occupied my Castle ... and where she went again after the brutal burning of my Castle'.[15]

Right
Katherine Everett, who moved into nearby Sybil Hill at the invitation of her cousin Olive Ardilaun after the latter was widowed in 1915.

Overleaf
St Anne's Park today, looking east towards the Howth peninsula. In the foreground are Benjamin Lee Guinness's walled garden and clock tower. The track beyond leads towards where the house stood.

3

ASHFORD CASTLE

County Mayo

Ashford Castle's setting is magical. It perches dramatically on the shore of Lough Corrib, which straddles the border between County Galway and County Mayo; and the views from the house stretch across formal gardens and pools to this, the second largest lake in Ireland after Lough Neagh. Lough Corrib is scattered with hundreds of tiny islands, once the refuge of saints and pirates. Ashford is, said one nineteenth-century writer, an 'oasis in this wild district, at once lovely, striking, and peculiar'.[1]

The house itself is a complicated building with a complicated building history, bearing out the verdict of Ireland's National Built Heritage Service that 'the castle presents a wide variety of features and styles which although apparently disparate in their forms, somehow come together to complement each other and create a structure which is unique in Ireland.'[2] The Anglo-Norman de Burgo family had a castle on the site in the thirteenth century, which was altered and further fortified in the sixteenth. A vaguely French residential block with dormer windows was added in the eighteenth century, but it fell into ruin under the Oranmore and Browne family, and Sir William Wilde, the father of Oscar, who had a summer retreat at nearby Moytura House, wrote in *Lough Corrib, Its Shores and Islands* (1867) how it was dilapidated and neglected, 'a very picture of poor Ireland herself when stricken by famine and pestilence'.[3] Ashford was rescued by Sir Benjamin Lee Guinness, who acquired it in 1852 via the Encumbered Estates' Court, which had been established three years earlier in the wake of the Great Famine to enable impoverished owners and their creditors to sell entailed estates. Benjamin Lee modernised the castle and added a new farmyard complex.

But the credit for turning Ashford into one of Ireland's great country houses must go to his son Arthur, Sir Arthur from 1868 and Lord Ardilaun from 1880. Ardilaun inherited the castle from his father along with nearly 20,000 acres in Galway and a further 3,266 in south Mayo; and after his

Opposite
Aerial view of Ashford Castle, with Lough Corrib beyond.

marriage in 1871 he and his wife Olive set about transforming the castle into a deliciously turreted, towered and battlemented concoction, a stunningly romantic neo-Gothic fantasy. His architect, for the early part of this work at least, was the maverick James Franklin Fuller, who also worked on St Anne's until the two men fell out. Fuller claimed the castellated additions to Ashford as his own work in his 1916 autobiography. After the rift, Ardilaun turned to George Coppinger Ashlin to complete the work, as he had at St Anne's.

Before being elevated to the nobility, Sir Arthur Guinness was usually described as being 'of Ashford', and when he introduced his new bride to the tenantry he spoke of bringing her 'to my old home', declaring that 'she comes, an Irishwoman, to live as such amongst you.'[4] In fact the couple didn't spend much time at the castle, although they did spend an awful lot of money on improving house and estate – around £2 million, according to one estimate. The interiors were the last word in opulent comfort. The reception rooms were panelled in oak, or in exotic foreign woods; the dining room ceiling was papered in Japanese gold. Ardilaun laid out formal gardens and planted a million trees, turning a wilderness

Below
The Oak Hall at Ashford Castle today.

Right
Chimneypiece at Ashford Castle.

into a paradise, and developing woodcock shooting over the estate until it was reckoned to be the best in the whole of the United Kingdom. He kept a steam yacht, the *Eglinton*, riding at anchor beneath the castle walls, ready to take house guests on a mini-cruise around the islands of Lough Corrib, which are scattered with early Christian ruins. As late as 1904 he was still adding to the house, installing a new billiard room and building garages for a fleet of motor cars. And he played with the idea of a castle. 'I have a taste for the picturesque,' he said, having built a tall viewing tower on the estate where he flew the Guinness family flag when he and Olive were at home.[5]

Two visitors to Ashford in the 1880s gave their impressions of the Ardilauns' castle. Gertrude Clements' husband had unexpectedly inherited the estates of the 3rd Earl of Leitrim after the earl was shot dead by disaffected tenants, and the couple came to Galway in May 1880 to meet with their tenants, many of whom were unable or unwilling to pay their rents following a hard winter and the efforts of the Land League, founded the previous year, to agitate against landlordism and to coordinate rent strikes in the west of Ireland. The Ardilauns were in England, celebrating Lord Ardilaun's elevation to the peerage; but Gertrude and her party were shown over the castle by his gamekeeper. She liked the setting, and admired the older parts of the building; the rest, she announced was 'too fanciful'.[6] And in what was to become a familiar refrain in any discussion of the Guinness family, she also commented on Ardilaun's great wealth, saying that he 'has money enough for any vagary and indulgence besides all that he spends so well and generously on the county'.[7]

Below
An 1879 portrait by Edouard Manet of George Moore, who stayed with Lord Ardilaun at Ashford Castle.

The author George Moore was also in Mayo and Galway in the early 1880s to look at the condition of his own estates. His uncle, who was also his agent, had written to him in Paris to say that as a result of the Land League campaign he was too scared to collect rents or serve eviction notices and that Moore had better come over and find himself another agent. While he was there, the Ardilauns invited him to spend a few days with them at Ashford.

Moore was impressed by the setting:

> Oh! The towers and battlements rising out of the benign foliage of ten thousand trees. The lake from where we stand looks like a girdle of pale grey silk bound about the green garments of the Emerald Isle: the long line of mountains upbreaking in jagged outlines, through a drift of clouds – now dark with storm, now resplendent with sunshine! And we lift the unsatiated eyes from this rapture of scenical loveliness.[8]

He revelled unashamedly in the comforts that Ashford had to offer – the house party gathering in the elegant long drawing room before dinner, or sitting down to breakfast in the oak room with fountains playing on the lawn, the joy of waking in a bedroom 'beautiful and bright with Indian curtains'.[9] But all the home comforts that money could buy couldn't keep the world out. Moore had been told before his visit that despite being active in creating jobs and relieving poverty on his estates, Ardilaun was unpopular – both because he was a Protestant and a Conservative, and because he was rich enough to withstand the Land League's rent strikes. 'Would you believe it, he is guarded by policemen in a place where he has spent thousands and thousands of pounds, where he has done more real good ... than perhaps any Irish man that ever lived?'[10] Now, as Moore sat down to breakfast he heard the sound of explosions and tiny splinters of stone spattered against the windows, as fifty or sixty men worked to blast a wide moat out of the solid rock connecting the castle to the mainland. Ardilaun joked that he was going to have cannon placed at convenient intervals on the battlements, and he would have a drawbridge which could be raised each night.

He was implacably opposed to self-government for Ireland (as were all the Guinnesses). This didn't endear him to nationalists. In 1872 he received an anonymous death threat, calling him an 'Orange whelp' and warning him that 'we have a person hired to shoot you'.[11] He promptly forwarded the letter to the *Daily Express* and asked them to reprint it, which they duly did. But compared to some, he was a good landlord. In December 1879, for example, he agreed to a rent reduction of between 20 and 30 percent to many of his smaller tenants, and he donated £3,000 for them to buy meal and seed potatoes. But – again, like most of the Guinnesses – he did not take kindly to resistance. Tenants who had opposed him were excluded from the rent abatement. He was also

Left
The shooting of Viscount Montmorres, as reported in *The Graphic*, 9 October 1880.

relentless in pursuing anyone who trespassed on his lands, prohibiting his tenants from keeping dogs so that the wildlife at Ashford wouldn't be disturbed, and routinely prosecuting anyone whom his keepers found with snares or traps on his land.

However, Ardilaun was a skilful strategist when it came to playing off different factions against each other. Unlike many major landlords in the west of Ireland, he made a point of not trying to control his tenants' voting preferences in parliamentary elections and – again in contrast to many of his fellow Protestants – he made a point of supporting the Catholic clergy, providing financial support for Catholic schools and churches. Father Patrick Lavelle, the local priest, came to his parish in 1869 with a reputation for fighting landlordism. Within a couple of years, he was dining regularly with the Ardilauns, who found him a parochial house, gave him a farm and, according to local people, paid off his debts. Nationalists were not impressed, although motives were mixed: opposition to Ardilaun's 'callous and heartless indifference to the ... well-being of the people' was led by Father Walter Conway, who was furious because Ardilaun hadn't funded repairs to his church, giving the money instead to Lavelle to build a new church.

The years 1879–82 were hard for tenants – and for landlords. And something more serious lay behind Ardilaun's joking reference to cannon and drawbridges. In June 1879 his agent, William Burke, narrowly escaped serious injury when Margaret Noonan, a woman he had recently evicted from her cottage, flung a bucket of boiling water in his face, and followed it up by throwing the bucket as well.* She was jailed for six months. In September the following year a neighbour of the Ardilauns, Viscount Mountmorres, was shot dead while driving alone to his home on the shores of Lough Corrib; and two years later, two of Lord Ardilaun's bailiffs were murdered as they tried to serve eviction notices on twelve of his tenants who were withholding their rents.

The Ardilauns entertained on a lavish scale at Ashford. They held a banquet in a temporary building in the grounds for 500 of their tenants and their families to celebrate their wedding, for example, (and commissioned a photographer to record the proceedings); and they welcomed quite a large house party several times a year, sometimes combining it with a ball for the local gentry. Lord Ardilaun usually brought down a shooting party for the woodcock season, which ran from January to 1 March. His coverts were famous, which was why in 1904 he was told to expect an important guest whose enthusiasm for shooting was legendary – none other than the Prince of Wales.

Ardilaun's brother Lord Iveagh was used to hobnobbing with royalty: Edward VII and the prince were regular visitors to Elveden, his shooting estate in Suffolk. And members of the royal family were occasional, if not frequent, visitors to Ireland. The king and queen had made an official

* The case was complicated, involving more than a simple eviction. Apparently, the tenant was a local man called Michael Hopkins who had lived in the cottage for forty years; his niece Margaret Noonan had moved in with her brother and both were refusing to leave. Hopkins appealed to Lord Ardilaun, who decided the simplest way to rectify the situation was to evict all three and then re-install Hopkins.

visit in 1903, and a private visit the following year, when they stayed with the Duke and Duchess of Devonshire at the Devonshires' Waterford seat, Lismore Castle. But the arrival of a royal guest was still a comparatively rare event in the west of Ireland, perhaps because of fears over security; and even though the prince's visit was classed as a private one, entertaining royalty was not something for the Ardilauns to take lightly. The visit to Ashford for a week's shooting was originally scheduled for December 1904, but it was put back to the New Year, so that the prince could be present for the start of the Dublin season at the end of January.

The Ardilauns spent Christmas and the New Year at Staunton Harold Hall in Leicestershire with Earl Ferrers and his wife, Lady Ardilaun's sister; but they were back at St Anne's in early January and then set off for Ashford to supervise the preparations. Lord Ardilaun had ordered extra furniture to be sent down for the prince's suite and the main reception rooms. He also had £45,000-worth of gold and silver plate brought in for use during the visit: it came in two special vans, guarded by private detectives.

The prince disembarked at Kingstown early on the morning of 24 January 1905. He was met by the Lord Lieutenant, the Earl of Dudley, who took him up to Dublin Castle by special train. After breakfast and lunch at the castle, the prince and his equerry, Sir Charles Cust, set out for Ballinrobe, the nearest station to Ashford, arriving there 20 minutes ahead of schedule, just before 4.00pm. Fortunately, Ardilaun was earlier still. He was waiting on the platform with an assortment of local dignitaries – the resident magistrate, the archdeacon of Tuam, one of the railway company directors – and after the prince had inspected a guard of honour which consisted of forty men of the Royal Irish Constabulary, he and Lord Ardilaun climbed into a waiting carriage and set off on the nine-mile drive to Cong and Ashford.

Several hundred people had gathered outside the station to see the heir to the throne and more came out to see the carriage as it passed. The press indulged in that patronising romanticisation of poverty that characterised so much thinking about the west of Ireland around the turn of the century. *The Daily Telegraph* reported that 'frequent groups of peasantry were encountered' on the road, 'the women and young girls lending a touch of colour to the scene with their bright petticoats'. The *Telegraph*'s reporters were also keen to stress the widespread expressions of loyalty and the absence of any threat to the prince: memories of the 1882 assassination in Phoenix Park of Lord Frederick Cavendish,

Opposite
It was Arthur and Olive Ardilaun who in the 1870s transformed Ashford into the neo-Gothic fantasy we see today.

Chief Secretary for Ireland and his Permanent Under-Secretary Thomas Burke were still relatively fresh. Driving from Dublin Castle to Broadstone railway station, the prince had been escorted by only three mounted policemen; and he and Lord Ardilaun travelled from Ballinrobe to Ashford in an open carriage, 'unattended by the regulation police escort'.[12] It was left to the nationalist *United Irishman* to mutter darkly that the royal visit was really part of a recruiting campaign to persuade local men to enlist in the British army.

It was dusk when the party neared Cong, but there were bonfires in the streets and candles burning in almost every cottage in the village. Ardilaun had arranged a twenty-one-gun salute in the park, there were steam yachts and sailing boats on the lough, and the drive to Ashford was lined with men carrying torches, who fell in behind the prince's carriage and escorted him up to the house. He had barely set foot inside the front door when he was invited to view one more spectacle: Ardilaun had arranged for coloured lights to play on the fountain on the lawn in front of the house, while estate workers lined up on the terrace with their torches and Francis Turnly, Ardilaun's agent, called for three cheers for his royal highness.

The shooting party was up and out at first light the next morning. There were eight guns, a mixed bunch. Besides the prince, Sir Charles Cust and Lord Ardilaun there was one of Ardilaun's Plunket relations, Lord Rathmore; the Earl of Bandon; Percy La Touche, a hunting squire from Kildare; the Hon. Robert Dillon, son of a previous Lord-Lieutenant

Below
House party at Ashford Castle, September or October 1880.

of Galway; and Major Arthur Acland-Hood, reckoned to be one of the greatest of all Edwardian shots.

Their quarry was the woodcock, a bird whose secretive habits and erratic flight pattern gave it more of a sporting chance than many game birds had. It also made it something of a challenge, even for experienced guns. The record bag on the Ashford estate, made in 1902, was 211 birds: a far cry from the 3,937 pheasants shot by a party including the prince, by then George V, at Hall Barn in Buckinghamshire on a single day, 18 December 1913. The bag on the prince's first day at Ashford was more modest still. The guns arrived at the first covert at 8.30am, accompanied by fifty beaters with dogs, who walked in a line making shrill cries and tapping the trees with long staves to stir the birds into flight. The bag for the day was 180 woodcock, and a few unlucky pheasants.

That was as good as it got for the week. Each day the party went out, sampling different coverts and ranging as far as Doon House, a shooting box owned by Lord Ardilaun and standing 12 miles from Ashford Castle. But they only managed twenty-nine woodcock and were left to admire the scenery, which was indeed breathtakingly beautiful. It included a group of bare-footed children who stood all day on a bleak, cold hill-top guarding a fluttering red banner bearing the words, 'God Bless the Prince.'

The relatively low fatality rate among Ashford's woodcock population notwithstanding, the Prince of Wales enjoyed his visit, and the Ardilauns considered it a success. As Lord Ardilaun left on the Tuesday morning to drive the prince to Ballinrobe, where a special train was waiting to take him on to Dublin, the beaters lined up outside the castle to give a cheer, and the route was decorated with flags and branches of evergreen. Tenants cheered and waved enthusiastically, said the newspapers. All the same, forty men from the Royal Irish Constabulary were there again at the station to meet the party; the prince personally congratulated the district inspector who had been in charge of security during the visit; and as the prince's train steamed out of the station to cheers from the assembled dignitaries, it was preceded by a pilot engine which had the task of ensuring that the line was clear and the rails had not been sabotaged.

By the following year, Lord Ardilaun had so far relaxed his antipathy towards trespassers as to open the gardens of Ashford Castle to the public. 'Ticket, obtained in village, must be presented *punctually* at 11 or 3,' noted *Black's Guide to Ireland*.[13]

4

FARMLEIGH

Dublin

The fashionable portrait painter William Orpen never forgot Farmleigh. Or to be more accurate, he never forgot his first visit there. Driven through Dublin in a motor car for the first time in his life, he sat rigid with terror in the back of the chauffeur-driven vehicle which bowled along the Quays westward and out into Phoenix Park. After the event he drew a characteristically self-deprecating sketch of himself in the back of the car, his mouth open in a soundless scream while onlookers pointed and stared at the unfamiliar sight of an automobile on the streets of Dublin.

It was 1904. Lord Iveagh had commissioned a portrait from Orpen, at a cost of £80, and he had sent his chauffeur to collect the artist for a

Opposite
The columned porte-cochère at Farmleigh's entrance.

Left
William Orpen's sketch of himself en route to Farmleigh for the first time.

sitting at Farmleigh. It was the first of many, and poor Orpen didn't have an easy time of it. The dreaded motor car would break down en route, making him late for appointments; then Lord Iveagh might be called away to a board meeting at the brewery, leaving the artist to kick his heels and tinker with the picture. When it was all but completed, Lord and Lady Iveagh did that thing which has sent shivers down the spine of every portrait painter since time began: they showed it to their friends and asked them what they thought of it. The consensus was that Orpen had made Iveagh's chin too long and his head too big. So he had to change it. 'This is a blow to me,' he wrote to his wife, 'as at present it is one of the best heads – if not the best – I have done.'[1]

The portrait, which *is* one of Orpen's best despite the tinkering, still hangs at Farmleigh. It shows a moustachioed Iveagh in half profile against a nondescript background, wearing a white waistcoat, wing collar and formal jacket. His greying hair is pushed back from a high forehead; his arms are folded; and he glances sideways at the spectator through sleepy, hooded eyes. But Orpen managed to capture something of the remoteness of the man, something which was neither arrogance nor hauteur, but more akin to shyness. The richest man in Ireland, and one of the richest men in the United Kingdom, seemed slightly surprised at his success.

And that success was astonishing. He began working in the family brewery when he was fifteen years old and although he was not yet twenty-one when his father, Benjamin Lee Guinness, died in 1868, he took on the management of the family brewery, ostensibly in partnership with his eldest brother Arthur, later Lord Ardilaun. But Arthur took little interest in the workings of the firm, while continuing to take the lion's share of the profits; after he sold his shares in 1876, Edward Cecil was left as sole proprietor. His decision in 1886 to float Guinness as a public company was a masterstroke, making him a millionaire overnight; and although he retired as managing director of Guinness in 1890 – marking his departure by placing in trust a quarter of a million pounds to be used to build worker housing in Dublin and London – he remained as chair of the board and continued to make all the major decisions over the management of the firm, and most of the minor ones, as well. His success in business coupled with his commitment to civic duty – at different times he was high sheriff of both Dublin city and Dublin county – his hefty donations to the Conservative Party and above all his public philanthropy all served to propel him up the social ladder. A baronetcy came in 1885, in

Opposite
Orpen's portrait of Edward Cecil Guinness, Lord Iveagh, 1904, which still hangs at Farmleigh.

recognition of his services in helping to arrange a visit to Ireland by the Prince of Wales. That was followed in 1891 by elevation to the peerage as Baron Iveagh of Iveagh, in County Down. He was made Viscount Iveagh in 1905 and Earl of Iveagh in 1919.

In May 1873 Edward Cecil married a distant cousin, Adelaide Guinness. He was 26, and she was three years older. She was the daughter of a father who was a bankrupt barrister and who had died back in 1857, and a mother who was the daughter of a baronet and who had pronounced views on suitable matches for her daughter – which was perhaps why Adelaide was still unmarried at 29. One of her mother's objections to the match with Edward Cecil was that if Adelaide married there would be 'nobody to exercise the dogs'.[2]

The marriage went ahead, dog-walkers or no dog-walkers, and it was an undoubted success. The newly-weds quickly established themselves as two of Dublin's brightest stars, entertaining the great and the good on a regular basis. In the year of their marriage, they bought the 78-acre Farmleigh estate on the edge of Phoenix Park, which had at its heart a modest Georgian country house. The location was perfect: a leisurely walk or drive through Phoenix Park would take Edward Cecil to the brewery, while his neighbours in the park included the Viceroy and the Chief Secretary for Ireland. Farmleigh put the Guinnesses close to the seat of power. They took possession on 29 September 1873, and they stayed there for the first time two weeks later.

Farmleigh was never more than an occasional semi-rural retreat: the couple's main residences were 80 St Stephen's Green and, after they took a lease on the property in 1877, 5 Grosvenor Place in London's Belgravia. But that didn't prevent them from transforming Farmleigh into a mansion which epitomised late-Victorian taste and grew to rival Lord Ardilaun's St Anne's on the other side of Dublin. They went to the Guinness family's architect of choice, James Franklin Fuller, who had not yet fallen out with Ardilaun. In 1874 Fuller was brought in to repair the existing outbuildings at Farmleigh, and an undated proposal labelled 'New Residence Farmleigh' and almost certainly by Fuller, suggests that his clients were at one stage considering sweeping away the two-storey Georgian house entirely and replacing it with a dramatically Jacobethan mansion, all gables and tall chimney stacks and spirelets.

Nothing came of this, however, and Edward Cecil, presumably with the agreement of Adelaide, opted instead for an enormous extension, retaining the slightly austere classicism of the original exterior. In 1880–1

Right
Farmleigh in 1873, the year it was bought by Edward Cecil Guinness.

Below right
The south front of the greatly extended house, pictured in 1900, after the ballroom had been added but before the glasshouse.

Bottom right
Ground-floor plan.
In pink is the original Georgian house, which after the extension housed the library, drawing room and Adelaide's boudoir. In green are the additions of 1880–1, including the entrance hall and dining room; and in blue, the 1897 ballroom and 1901 glasshouse.

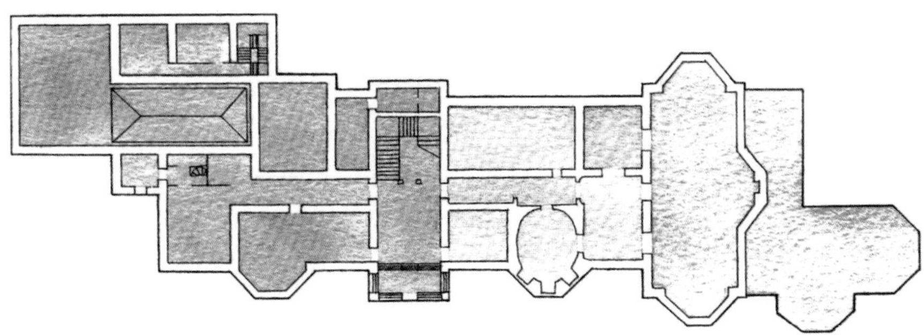

Fuller doubled the size of the house by building a replica (externally, at least) of the original to the west, and connecting the two with a new pedimented entrance hall which was reached via that most Victorian of architectural features, a columned porte-cochère. Kitchens and domestic offices were hidden away on the north side behind the new block. Adelaide's realm, an oval boudoir and two drawing rooms, was in the old part of the house. There was an oak-panelled smoking room, and a top-lit billiard room lined with striking red cotton for the men, and a huge library, although in a break with convention this last seems to have been a gender-neutral space rather than the usual male preserve. Edward Cecil had a suite of his own, comprising a study with its own entrance, so that visitors who came on business didn't have to walk through the house; and a first-floor dressing room and bedroom, with their own staircase. A stone stair concealed behind a false bookcase led down from the study to Edward Cecil's personal strong room, one of two in the basement, both of which had steel doors and granite surrounds.

Below
The entrance hall.

Right
The billiard room.

The new rooms at Farmleigh were decorated with a heady mix of seventeenth-, eighteenth- and nineteenth-century furnishings and art objects, from neo-Renaissance carving in the library to Rococo plasterwork in one of the two drawing rooms and Victorian statues in the entrance hall. Some of the decoration was provided by the London firm of Charles Mellier & Co., who described themselves as interior decorators, upholsterers, cabinet makers and dealers in works of art and who also worked for the Rothschilds. Mellier & Co. mixed antiques and reproduction furniture from different periods and in different styles to give interiors which, while they may have been historically rather bewildering, were

Above
View of the entrance hall from the grand staircase.

undeniably opulent and thus in keeping with their time. The firm seems to have become involved at Farmleigh initially when Edward Cecil and Adelaide decided to hang four late seventeenth-century Italian embroideries which they had bought at auction in London in 1874. Depicting Jupiter, Saturn and Venus from a series called *The Seven Planetary Gods*, and Africa from a separate set, *The Four Parts of the World*, the panels had once belonged to Queen Maria Cristina de Borbón, who acted as regent after the death of her husband Ferdinand VII of Spain in 1833 – a royal connection which delighted the Iveaghs. Mellier & Co. placed these seventeenth-century Italian embroideries with a nineteenth-century Spanish provenance in a setting redolent of eighteenth-century France. It isn't clear what other contributions Mellier & Co. made to Farmleigh,

Above
The dining room, featuring sumptuous decorations by C. Mellier & Co., including life-sized nude statues either side of the Italian tapestry.

but their inscribed lockplates in the study and the smoking room show that their work certainly extended beyond the dining room.

Edward Cecil and Adelaide's household at Farmleigh was substantial, to say the least, especially considering that the mansion was only used occasionally. According to the 1901 census they kept thirty-five servants, which was a lot even for those more opulent times. There were twelve women, ranging in age from a forty-three-year-old housekeeper, Frances Edwards, down to sixteen-year-old Helen Wilkie, whose role at Farmleigh was unspecified but who was presumably a tweenie or a scullery maid. The menservants, all twenty-three of them, included four liveried footmen, a 'motor car driver' – perhaps the same chauffeur who was to terrify poor William Orpen – an engineer, and half a dozen 'stable helpers'. The roles of the other male servants weren't identified on the census return; but there was a fashion for continental 'man cooks', so the only Frenchman in the household, Antoine De Clat, may well have been the Iveaghs' chef. We know that twenty years later they employed a Neapolitan chef, August De Luca, at Elveden, their Suffolk country house.

But the most intriguing feature of the Iveaghs' Farmleigh household was that only one of the servants, a stable helper from Kildare called John Murphy, was Irish: the other thirty-four were all English, Scots or in De Clat's case, French. And with the exception of Murphy and De Clat, both Roman Catholics, the entire household was Protestant. Edward Cecil and Adelaide gave their religion as Church of Ireland; and there were two Scottish Presbyterians. Everyone else identified as Church of England. Ardent Unionists though the Iveaghs were, like all of the Guinness clan at the time, this seems to have been taking things a little too far, although it was not particularly unusual in the Anglocentric and increasingly polarised society of Ireland in the early twentieth century. One wishes one knew more about the Iveaghs' recruitment practices. Did they advertise in one of the big London agencies, Mrs Hunt's or Mrs Massey's? (Impossibly, the latter is still going strong today and advertising itself as 'the world's oldest private household agency'.[3]) Most of their household would have moved with them between Farmleigh and the house on St Stephen's Green, but did they also move between Ireland and England? Or did Edward Cecil maintain several households simultaneously, an enormous extravagance when the annual wage bill for a household this size ran to around £1,000, as much as half a million at today's values? Some of the servants certainly travelled: in 1921, when the Iveaghs were entertaining at Elveden, George Cain, who had been a kitchen porter at Farmleigh in 1901, was with them. He was the only servant whose name appears in both the 1901 and 1921 censuses, however, suggesting that either some of the others remained in Ireland (or at the Grosvenor Place house); or that the Iveaghs weren't very good at keeping their staff.

In 1897 Edward Cecil and Adelaide, who were now entertaining on an increasingly lavish scale, decided they needed more social space at Farmleigh; and they commissioned an enormous new ballroom from the Scottish-born, London-based architect William Young who also worked for them at St Stephen's Green and Elveden. Young seems to have worked with the established Edinburgh firm of Morison & Co., 'decorative contractors, cabinet makers, upholsterers, billiard table makers &c' who were best known at the time for fitting out luxury railway carriages.[4] They supplied the portières or formal curtains that framed the windows, giving a touch of eighteenth-century France to the room; and they may also have advised on the low-relief plasterwork, which also nods to the France of Louis XVI. Unusually for Ireland, the plaster detail was applied to timber panelling, and the whole painted white. The ballroom filled the full width of the house, front to back, with projecting bay windows at each end. It gave onto Farmleigh's two drawing rooms, but there was also a corridor running through the original house all the way from the entrance hall, so that guests arriving for a dance didn't have to pass through the state rooms.

Right
The ballroom, decorated in the style of 18th-century France.

The new ballroom at Farmleigh made its public debut on the evening of Tuesday 17 April 1900. A visit to Ireland by the eighty-year-old Queen Victoria that month was the occasion for a round of dinners and concerts and balls, all involving the *haut*-est of Dublin's *haut monde*. The queen was staying at the Viceregal Lodge in Phoenix Park (now Áras an Uachtaráin, the official residence of the presidents of Ireland), and the Iveaghs were her guests for an intimate dinner on Monday 16 April, in a party of fourteen that included two of the queen's daughters, Princess Christian of Schleswig-Holstein and Princess Henry of Battenberg, the Archbishop of Armagh, and the Lord Lieutenant of Ireland and his wife, Earl and Countess Cadogan, who had decamped to Dublin Castle for the duration of the royal visit. (That was one up for the Iveaghs on Lady Ardilaun being allowed to hand the queen a bunch of primroses as she drove by St Anne's.)

The following night the queen's third son, the Duke of Connaught, who had recently been appointed military Commander-in-Chief, Ireland, hosted a concert for 450 which was hailed as 'the most brilliant social event that has occurred since the queen's arrival'.[5] It took place not at the duke and duchess's official residence, the Royal Hospital at Kilmainham, but in the new ballroom at Farmleigh, which had been lent to them by Lord and Lady Iveagh while Kilmainham was being redecorated.

Farmleigh was 'an altogether ideal residence for a great reception', commented one British newspaper, noting the 'numerous unrivalled pieces of old English and Irish furniture' in evidence throughout the house.[6] The Iveaghs' gardeners outdid themselves, with masses of flowers everywhere. Clusters of arum lilies and palms filled every corner of the ballroom, and the platform for the royal party (complete with gold chairs) was banked up with maidenhair ferns and meadowsweet and festooned with silk flags from the royal yacht *Victoria and Albert*.

Queen Victoria didn't attend the Connaughts' concert, but everyone else did, from Princess Christian and Princess Henry to the Cadogans, Arthur Balfour, Chief Secretary for Ireland – and the Iveaghs, who brought a party which included three countesses and a Prussian diplomat, Count Paul Metternich. In contrast to the colourful decorations, both those which filled the ballroom and those which filled the bemedalled chests of the various military men in their dress uniforms, the women seem to have opted for a monochrome look. The Duchess of Connaught wore diamonds, pearls, and oyster-white satin; Princess Christian wore black; and Countess Cadogan wore grey brocade, trimmed with lace. 'Lady Iveagh's diamonds were remarkably fine', noted *The Daily Telegraph*'s Dublin correspondent.[7] The programme included works by Mendelssohn, Chopin, Gounod (*Ave Maria*) and Bizet; and a virtuoso performance by the Dutch violinist Johannes Wolff. But the celebrated mezzo-soprano Blanche Marchesi was the star of the show. According to the British press, she 'held her audience enthralled by her intensely dramatic singing of Schubert's *Erl Konig*'.[8] It was well after midnight before the royal party retired to the Farmleigh dining room for supper and the rest of the guests made their way home.

The year after the Connaughts' concert, the Iveaghs decided on yet another extension to Farmleigh – that most Edwardian of country house adjuncts, a conservatory, which was to be built immediately to the east of the new ballroom. On the advice of Clyde Young, who had taken over his father William's architectural practice on the latter's death in 1900, the Iveaghs went to the engineering firm of Mackenzie and Moncur, of Edinburgh, Glasgow and London.

Mackenzie and Moncur came with the best references. They were 'hothouse builders and heating engineers' to Edward VII by royal warrant, and the list of patrons in their 1901 prospectus consisted of 200 names, all titled, beginning with the recently deceased Queen Victoria, her son and grandson, and included nine dukes, seven marquises and no fewer than thirty earls.[9] Their products ranged from boilers and radiators, cold frames, bandstands and cricket pavilions to big, utilitarian hothouses and elaborately curvaceous concoctions in iron and glass; and while most of their work was in Scotland and the north of England – in 1896 they designed the fabulous palm house at Sefton Park in Liverpool – they did make the occasional foray into Ireland. In the 1880s, for example, M. & M., as they called themselves, constructed a range of glasshouses on the Jameson estate at Malahide, north of Dublin; and in the 1890s they supplied an elaborate palm room for a family of well-known horse breeders, the Hollwey Steeds, at Clonsilla Lodge, a couple of miles north-west of Farmleigh.

At Farmleigh M. & M. constructed a delightful bubble of light, all curves and semi-domes framed in a mixture of steel and timber which still has the power to charm the visitor today. The L-shaped conservatory led directly out of the new ballroom, a fragile climax to all the Iveaghs'

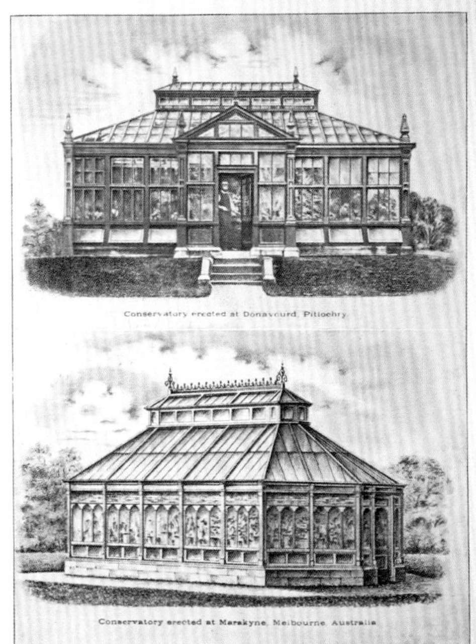

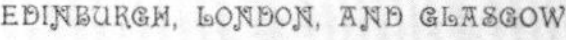

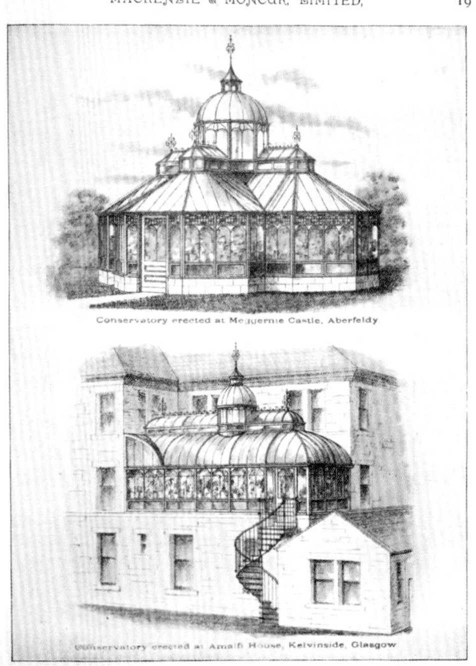

new work on their house; and it is easy to picture it in its heyday, when it was filled with orchids and heavily scented exotic blooms, the perfect spot for the kind of assignation which loomed so large in a hundred Edwardian novels, as star-crossed lovers left off their dancing and sought privacy behind the palms.

Time hasn't been kind to big country house conservatories. Their natural fragility coupled with high heating bills and a scarcity of labour has meant that too many have been lost. That makes the survival of the Farmleigh conservatory all the more remarkable. And even more precious.

Above
Pages from M. & M.'s catalogue, with examples of glasshouses they had designed from Scotland to Australia.

Opposite
Adelaide Guinness reclines in the conservatory at Farmleigh, in a painting by the society portraitist George Elgar Hicks, 1885.

Overleaf
The south front in springtime.

INTERLUDE: THE HOUSES OF GOD

Most members of the Guinness clan maintained an unwavering commitment to Protestantism and the Church of Ireland. The first Arthur Guinness had an evangelical streak in him, although unsurprisingly he didn't think much of that mainstay of evangelical Protestantism, temperance. His son, Arthur II, was also devout, always keeping his Bible by him and routinely inviting guests and business acquaintances to pray with him.

Like many a nineteenth-century magnate who indulged themselves by building palatial mansions, the next two generations of Guinnesses salved their consciences and saved their souls by also building churches. Lord Ardilaun commissioned George C. Ashlin to build a new church on the edge of the St Anne's estate for the Protestant parishioners of Raheny; in a move characteristic of Guinness philanthropy, he was both generous and controlling. He contributed to the endowment of the parish, but stipulated that in return, he must have the right of presenting a rector. The new church was opened in 1889, and Ardilaun's wife Olive continued to support it after her husband's death, donating a new organ in 1919 (at a cost of £800) in memory of her husband and commissioning new stained-glass windows in memory of other family members. In 1902 Ardilaun's brother, the 1st Earl of Iveagh, commissioned W.D. Caroë to rebuild the little church of St Andrew and St Patrick which served his English country house, Elveden in Suffolk. And their father, Benjamin Lee Guinness, restored St Mary's, the estate church at Ashford Castle, in the early 1860s.

All three Guinnesses were vehemently opposed to calls for the disestablishment of the Church of Ireland; although that had more to do with Unionism than with religion. Nevertheless, after the Irish Church Act of Disestablishment came into force in 1871, forcing the Church of Ireland to support itself without the benefit of tithes, both Ardilaun and Iveagh were quick to offer financial support.

However, it was Benjamin Lee who was responsible for the Guinness family's most famous contribution to the Church of Ireland's

Above
All Saints' Church, which Lord Ardilaun built for Raheny parish on his St Anne's estate.

Right
The church of St Andrew and St Patrick, Elveden, rebuilt by Lord Iveagh.

Above
St Mary's Church at Ashford Castle, Cong, restored by Benjamin Lee Guinness.

architectural heritage. By the nineteenth century, the medieval St Patrick's, one of Dublin's two Church of Ireland cathedrals, was in a sorry state. Surrounded by slum tenements, there were cracks in the walls, some of the vaulting had collapsed, and the south wall of the nave was leaning dangerously. A report of 1805 recommended demolishing the cathedral and starting again.

That didn't happen, but by the middle of the nineteenth century it was clear that something must be done if St Patrick's wasn't to fall into ruin. In 1846 the English architect Richard Cromwell Carpenter put forward a comprehensive scheme for restoring the cathedral at a cost of £100,000, but although work began on the Lady Chapel, the devastation caused by the Great Famine meant that fundraising for anything other than the alleviation of suffering was impossible, and most of the work was incomplete when Carpenter died in 1855.

At this point Benjamin Lee Guinness stepped in. In 1859 he went to the dean and chapter with an offer of £20,000 to fund the restoration of the cathedral, a demonstration of his commitment to the threatened national status of the Church of Ireland. There was one unusual condition: he was to be in charge of the works, effectively acting as his own architect while relying heavily on his own contractors, the Murphy brothers of Amiens Street in Dublin.

That raised a few eyebrows; but since no one else was offering to fund the project, Benjamin Lee's offer was accepted. By June 1860 the nave had been screened off from the choir with a timber paling that reached up to the roof and scaffolding had been put up to support the roof, while the south wall, the flying buttresses which were holding it in place and the south transept were taken down preparatory to being rebuilt. Photographs were taken of stonework which was going to be lost in the restoration work, an early example of cameras being used to record architectural detail for a building project.

Below
St Patrick's Cathedral, Dublin, dramatically restored in the 1860s by Benjamin Lee Guinness, and pictured here in an 1890s Photochrome print.

As the work progressed, swiftly exceeding the optimistic £20,000 estimate, and praise poured in for Benjamin Lee's generosity (and, incidentally, for the fact that he insisted on employing Irish workers and craftsmen), one or two dissident voices began to be heard. Chief among them was James Joseph McCarthy, one of Ireland's leading Gothicists and a prolific church architect himself. McCarthy worked on four Irish cathedrals in his career, at Armagh, Monaghan, Derry and Thurles in County Tipperary, and he clearly thought he ought to be working on this one. He was not an easy man – he was once convicted of assault after slapping one of his apprentices across the face 'for looking cross' – and in a long letter to the *Dublin Builder* he let rip with his critique of Benjamin Lee's work at St Patrick's.[1]

Enraged that such an important project should be 'left in the hands of an amateur, and of builders and tradesmen', McCarthy argued that it would be better to resurrect Carpenter's scheme for the cathedral. As it was, Benjamin Lee's team had failed to understand the importance of historical precedent and missed a splendid opportunity:

> Works of the last three centuries have been religiously restored in all their hideous deformity, while original and perfect works of the earlier and better period have been ruthlessly destroyed to make way for unauthorized and unnecessary features.

He went on to list the mistakes. The medieval rood screen had been removed to open up the view (and he did have a point here – its loss was to be regretted). Medieval corbel shafts were being replaced with shafts 'of gross proportions and coarse details'. The stone carvers were allowed to design the foliage adorning new capitals. Old buttresses were taken down to make way for imitations 'of the weakest, worst, and feeblest Tudor architecture.'[2] And so it went on.

McCarthy's was not the only voice raised in anger against Benjamin Lee's restoration. *The Daily Telegraph* called it 'naked, cold and cheerless'.[3] The Ecclesiological Society, unbending arbiter of taste when it came to all things medieval and liturgical, criticised Benjamin Lee for relying on himself as his own architect, rather than 'giving the opportunity to some leader of the ecclesiological school'.[4] As the work went on, the Society went further, condemning his repositioning of the stalls in the choir as 'a deplorably bad arrangement', declaring that the 'well-meant, but most deplorable, restoration of St Patrick's continues to excite the deep regrets of all ecclesiologists', and denouncing the 'deplorable ignorance' of Benjamin Lee and his builders when it came to appreciating the nature of the Gothic'.[5] ('Deplorable' was one of the Ecclesiologists' favourite words.) By the end of 1864 it was being reported that he had banned the Society from visiting the site, while the *Freeman's Journal* dismissed the Ecclesiologists as Pickwickian dilettanti.

Wisely, Benjamin Lee stayed out of the fight. Not so his contractors, the Murphy brothers, who launched a bitter attack in the *Freeman's Journal* on McCarthy's own record of designing 'dismal details', 'clumsy and absurd incongruities' and 'melancholy structure[s]'.[6] Nor his chief

Below
The reopening of St Patrick's Cathedral, as depicted in the *Illustrated London News* on 3 March 1865.

stonecutter, Thomas Read, who wrote at length in the *Dublin Builder* of McCarthy's failure to understand the basic principles of medieval stone carving, which had always given freedom to carvers to indulge their creative side. Other supporters pointed out that while not every detail was a perfect and scholarly example of the Gothic Revival, the alternative would have been to let the building fall down. And this is perhaps the most sensible verdict.

Through it all Benjamin Lee stood his ground, confident in his own abilities. On St Patrick's Day 1863 the workmen presented him with a specially composed ode, printed on white satin and filled with good will, if a little short on literary merit:

> Live on, St Patrick's, live, and may that generous heart
> That rescued you, be aye enshrined in that great work of art.[7]

The work was not completed for another two years, by which time the cost had risen to a colossal £150,000, well over £20 million at today's values. It was met almost entirely by Benjamin Lee. That was a remarkable achievement, and one which was acknowledged at the lavish reopening, which took place on 3 March 1865 in front of the Archbishop of Dublin, the Lord Mayor, the Lord-Lieutenant and a small army of nobles, gentry and clergy. It was the greatest work ever accomplished by a single citizen, declared the press. Benjamin Lee got a baronetcy, and in 1875, seven years after his death, a statue by the talented Dublin sculptor John Henry Foley, which still stands in the churchyard of St Patrick's today. It depicts him seated and deep in thought, his chin resting on his hand. Inscriptions on a simple plinth inform the passer-by that this is Sir Benjamin Lee Guinness, and that 'St Patrick's Cathedral was by him restored AD 1865.'

There are worse ways to be remembered.

Opposite
John Henry Foley's statue of Benjamin Lee Guinness in the churchyard of St Patrick's Cathedral.

SIR BENJAMIN LEE GUINNESS
BARONET LLD
MEMBER OF PARLIAMENT
FOR THE CITY OF DUBLIN

5
80 ST STEPHEN'S GREEN

Dublin

Number 80 St Stephen's Green, better known today as Iveagh House and for seventy years the Guinness family's Dublin town house, was built in 1736 for Dr Robert Clayton, a worldly Protestant cleric who was successively bishop of Killala, of Cork and of Clogher.

None of these appointments detained him for long in his pursuit of good living. 'He has travelled beyond the Alps,' reported the Earl of Orrery to a friend in 1737, and 'has brought home with him, to the amazement of our mercantile Fraternity, the Arts and Sciences that are the Ornament of Italy ... He eats, drinks and sleeps in taste'.[1] Bishop Clayton's translation to the see of Cork in 1735 prompted him to build himself a fine town house in Dublin, employing the services of Richard Castle, the German-born architect who was then at the beginning of a career which would see him become the greatest eighteenth-century exponent of Palladianism in Ireland, architect of Leinster House, now the seat of Dáil Éireann (1745–51), Carton House (1739–45) and Dublin's Lying-in Hospital, the Rotunda (1750–7), which was criticised at the time for looking more like a nobleman's palace than a hospital.[2]

For Clayton, Castle designed a palazzo of a town house, three bays wide and three storeys high over a basement, with a rusticated ground floor behind a flat-roofed Tuscan portico and a piano nobile largely taken up by a high-ceilinged great room. It was an unusually imposing building, and a striking addition to the houses scattered around St Stephen's Green. Lord Orrery, who visited when it was still a building site, was impressed, congratulating Clayton on his 'palace' and declaring that 'I even admire your coal cellars.'[3] His only concern was that Castle was placing the stables so close to the house, that the smell would interfere

Opposite
The north front entrance of 80 St Stephen's Green, Dublin.

Above
Dr Robert Clayton, who built 80 St Stephen's Green, portrayed with his wife Katherine by James Latham, *ca.*1740.

with the bishop's enjoyment of his palace. His proposed solution was for Clayton either to buy more land behind the house or to fill his garden with sweet-smelling flowers.

When Edward Cecil Guinness inherited 80 St Stephen's Green from his father Benjamin Lee in 1868, the house had already been altered several times. In the later eighteenth century, it was bought by Viscount Mountcashel, Earl Mountcashel from 1781, who commissioned decorative plasterwork and removed Castle's flat-roofed Tuscan portico, which had become rather too tempting a target for lead thieves. But the most dramatic changes were the work of Benjamin Lee himself. After buying the house through the Encumbered Estates Court in 1856 for a knock-down price of £2,500, in 1862 he acquired the lease of the house next door, 81, knocked *that* down and built an extension on the site which effectively doubled the size of Clayton's original palazzo. As with St Patrick's Cathedral, he acted as his own architect; and very competent he was, creating a series of neo-Georgian living rooms behind a unified classical façade of Portland stone, with a new portico and a pediment containing his baronet's arms and the family motto, *Spes mea in Deo*, 'My hope is in God'.

But the Guinnesses weren't finished with their St Stephen's Green palazzo yet. In 1880–1 Edward Cecil commissioned the family's favourite if difficult architect, John Franklin Fuller, who by now had worked on, or was working at, St Anne's, Ashford Castle, Farmleigh (and, incidentally, Lord Ardilaun's own Dublin town house, 18 Lower Leeson Street), to rebuild 79, on the other side of Benjamin Lee's extension, linking it to Clayton's original house and creating some pleasant period rooms. The most notable of these was the Adam Room which, if it didn't owe very much to the work of Robert Adam, was nonetheless light, airy and a good example of the Victorians' take on neoclassicism. Three years later Fuller rebuilt 78 St Stephen's Green to form a symmetrical pair with 79.

This work turned 80 into a colossal house. There was a bachelor's wing, accommodation for twenty live-in servants, and twenty-three

Right
One of the elaborate fireplaces installed at 80 St Stephen's Green.

principal bedrooms. But it still was not big enough for Edward Cecil and Adelaide. In 1896, at the same time as he was adding a ballroom to Farmleigh, the architect William Young created another in the garden behind 79, again using Morison & Co., the Edinburgh firm of decorative contractors who were working on the Farmleigh ballroom.

The result, which was reputed to cost a colossal £30,000 is wonderfully, outrageously, deliciously opulent, an outstanding example of late-Victorian and Edwardian taste and one of the most striking social spaces in Ireland. Measuring 60ft long by 35ft wide by 40ft high, it is dominated by a vast shallow dome. The walls are panelled in Algerian onyx, Carrara marble and Irish alabaster. The window hangings, by Morison & Co., are of red damask with strapwork in gold thread and appliqued sprays of flowers in silk. An alabaster chimneypiece has a vaguely Jacobethan look to it; the plasterwork decoration, by the Dublin firm of Darcy's, smacks of sixteenth-century Italian Mannerism; the seating for guests to sit out between dances references the early eighteenth century and the Régence of Philippe II, duc d'Orleans. It should be all too much, but it works brilliantly.

Below
The opulent ballroom at 80 St Stephen's Green, in an 1899 photograph from the Earl of Iveagh's family album.

Right
The grand staircase.

Although Farmleigh was only on the other side of Phoenix Park, 80 St Stephen's Green was the Iveaghs' primary residence when they were in Ireland, and it was where they did most of their entertaining during the Dublin season, which ran from early January to St Patrick's Day, 17 March. They were present at the vice-regal 'drawing rooms' at Dublin Castle which were a key feature of the season; they did the round of balls and receptions which were part of it. At the same time, everyone agreed that Edward Cecil was no socialite, remarking that he was quiet and reserved. Adelaide seems to have been the prime mover behind the couple's socialising. 'There is nothing about [Edward Cecil's] personality in the least suggestive of his ability to pay a million of money for any luxury he particularly fancied,' said the *Tatler*.[4] Kate Devereux, who as a maid to one of their family friends, Elizabeth Burke-Plunkett, Countess of Fingall, was a frequent visitor to the Iveaghs' homes, recalled that they lived like royalty, 'very grand, and very simple in their tastes'.[5]

Simplicity is relative. As a young debutante, Lady Clodagh Beresford, daughter of the 5th Marquess of Waterford, was a regular at their dances and at the dinners they gave beforehand. She remembered that those dinners were often impossibly crowded affairs: Adelaide couldn't bear to leave anyone out, and so her table, long though it was, was never quite long enough and dinner guests sat elbow-to-elbow. It was so difficult that partners would take it in turns, one sitting back while the other ate. Countess Fingall remembered a similar experience in 1904, when Edward VII and Queen Alexandra came to Ireland and were guests at a dinner held for them by the Iveaghs. Fifty waiters were hired for the occasion, and the table was so crowded, she claimed, 'that my neighbour and I made an agreement with each other to eat alternate courses'.[6]

On another occasion when Lady Fingall was staying with the Iveaghs in Stephen's Green, she was called upon to act as hostess at a big party, Adelaide being indisposed. As a reward, she was given Adelaide's pearls to wear for the night. 'I felt wrapped about in light,' she said, 'as though, if I had had nothing else on, I should still have been clothed, wearing them.'[7] But when the party ended, Edward Cecil didn't invite her to hand the pearls to a servant to put away: instead, he personally conducted her down to the cellar where, by the light of a candle, he took them from her and locked them away in a safe. One is reminded of the personal strong room in the basement at Farmleigh, reached by a concealed stair in Edward Cecil's study, and the fact that riches could bring with them a sense of insecurity. In normal circumstances Adelaide, who kept two personal maids, always put away her own jewellery – and, more unusually for someone in her position, she put away her own clothes, too.

Nor was the fear of theft entirely misplaced. Edward Cecil kept night watchmen in his houses: one of these, an ex-policeman named Cassidy, was on patrol one night at the Grosvenor Place house when he heard a noise and, going to investigate, found a burglar with his pockets full of antique silver trying to get out of the front door. He had come in through an open dining room window: why he didn't leave by the same route is not clear. After a brief struggle the thief, 'a tall, well-dressed man of gentlemanly appearance', was subdued and carted off to the police station where, in addition to the silver, he was found to have a gold snuff box, and a gold casket which had been a present from Prince Ferdinand of Bulgaria. All in all the gentlemanly burglar, who had only recently been released from gaol after being convicted of 'being unlawfully possessed of burglars' implements', had taken nearly £500 worth of items. He got twelve months' hard labour.[8]

The ambitious scale of Lord and Lady Iveagh's entertaining was set quite early on, while they were still plain Mr and Mrs Guinness and nearly two decades before William Young's huge ballroom echoed to the sounds of Casano's or one of the other fashionable Edwardian orchestras playing waltzes and quadrilles. In January 1881, at the height of the season, rumours began to circulate that Adelaide was planning a costume ball for around a thousand guests at 80 St Stephen's Green. No one in modern dress was to be admitted; no modern uniforms were allowed. The date set was Tuesday 10 February, and for weeks beforehand Dublin society was awash with rumours about who was wearing what, who was invited – and who was not. 'Mrs Guinness's ball has been for three weeks the one, the universal, the absorbing, the all-important topic,' declared the *Whitehall Review*. 'It has murdered sleep for many an aspirant to fashion, for not to be invited was social damnation.'[9]

When the day of the ball came, so did the cream of Dublin's *haut monde*, happily embracing Adelaide's demand that everyone must dress for the occasion. Earl Cowper, the Lord Lieutenant, came as a Venetian nobleman from the sixteenth century; his countess was a Venetian lady. Adelaide dressed as Madame de Pompadour in a white sacque-back gown embroidered in gold and a powdered wig. Edward Cecil started out as a Florentine nobleman, and changed to a cavalier halfway through the evening.

It must have been a magical sight. The staircases and passageways were filled with ferns and palms and curiously costumed figures. There were Chinese mandarins and cavaliers and fairies, matadors and Elizabethans and powdered ladies of the *ancien régime*. Two sisters came in white muslin as characters from a painting by Sir Joshua Reynolds; Major Hugh McCalmont, who had served in the Afghan Wars, dressed as a turbaned chieftain. The Countess of Drogheda was Old Mother Hubbard. There were two Portias.

By the early years of the twentieth century dinners and receptions and balls at 80 St Stephen's Green were an accepted part of the Dublin season. Lady Iveagh in satin and diamonds was a familiar sight – to Dublin's elite, at least – standing to receive her guests at the head of the marble staircase which led to William Young's flower-filled ballroom, or dancing the opening quadrille with her husband, the Lord Lieutenant and his wife.

But the Iveaghs didn't confine their entertaining to the house. They also made good use of 80's startlingly extensive grounds, which were

Right
Photo-montage of the costume ball at 80 St Stephen's Green on 10 February 1881.

Opposite
Edward Cecil Guinness dressed as a Louis XIII-period gentleman at another costume ball, July 1897.

more of a park than a garden. (And they are indeed a public park today: Iveagh Gardens is one of Dublin's nicest.) The 15-acre Coburg Gardens, behind 80 St Stephen's Green, had been acquired by Benjamin Lee Guinness in 1862 and leased to the Dublin Exhibition Palace and Winter Garden Company, as part of a Guinness-backed scheme to hold a show along the lines of the International Exhibition of Industries and Arts held in South Kensington that year. The grounds were laid out by the eminent landscape designer Ninian Niven, who seems to have decided that more is more: he created a maze, a 3-acre archery ground, parterres, rockeries, ponds and fountains and a 20 ft-high rustic grotto as a setting for the exhibition buildings, the most imposing of which was an enormous iron and glass palace, designed by the Dublin architect Alfred G. Jones . The exhibition, which was opened by the Prince of Wales in May 1865, was a great success, attracting nearly a million visitors.

Above
Contemporary print of the iron-and-glass palace built for the 1865 Dublin International Exhibition in Coburg Gardens.

But plans for a permanent exhibition site foundered, the Dublin Exhibition Palace and Winter Garden Company went bankrupt, and in 1870 Edward Cecil and his brother Arthur took the site back. They made another attempt to establish a permanent venue in the gardens with the 1872 Dublin Exhibition of Irish Arts, Industries and Manufactures; but again, the scheme failed, not least because of criticism that in a show of Irish products rather too many of the exhibitors were English; and in 1883 Edward Cecil sold the exhibition buildings to the Commissioners of Public Works for use by the new Royal University of Ireland.

But he kept the gardens, and he and Adelaide often allowed charitable events to take place there, whether they were in residence or not. In June 1887, for example, they hosted the summer show of the Royal Horticultural Society. 'The spacious marquees were filled with some of the most rare and lovely products of the floral and vegetable kingdom,' said the *Freeman's Journal*. 'And the still summer air was laden with the most exquisite perfume.'[10] The sun shone, military bands from the Prince of Wales' Own Regiment and the 4th Royal Irish Dragoons played 'God Save the Queen' and 'God Bless the Prince of Wales'; and crowds gathered outside the gardens for a glimpse of the guests of honour, Prince Albert Victor and his brother Prince George, sons of the Prince and Princess of Wales, who were accompanied around the exhibits by the Lord Lieutenant, the Marquess of Londonderry, and a troop of noblemen and other dignitaries. The newspaper reports made no mention of the Iveaghs being present, but they often travelled abroad in the summer, returning in time for Cowes Week in August. But Adelaide offered a special Jubilee prize (it was Queen Victoria's golden jubilee year) in three categories: best new rose, best hybrid and best tea or noisette bloom. All three were won by the County Down rose breeders, Alexander Dickson and Son. Edward Cecil got a Highly Commended in the 'Miscellaneous' section for his palms.

In 1899, the military bands would be playing again as men marched off to fight the Boers. Edward Cecil paid for and sent a fully equipped field hospital with space for a hundred men (and four officers) to South Africa, staffed by sixty-odd orderlies and three Dublin surgeons led by Sir William Thomson, a past president of the Royal College of Surgeons in Ireland and a future honorary surgeon to Edward VII. Known as the Irish Hospital, it sailed from London's Albert Dock on 3 February 1900, after being personally inspected by Edward Cecil, who presented the officers with wrist watches and the men with pipes and tobacco. Although it came under military command, Edward Cecil had paid for it and characteristically, he expected to retain a degree of control. The War Office, for example, objected to his plan to send two nurses with the hospital, saying it was against regulations. The War Office lost.

Also in 1899, Frank Benson's famous acting company performed *As You Like It* in the gardens of 80 St Stephen's Green, with Benson as Orlando – his fellow actors complained that he always kept the best parts for himself – and his wife Constance as Rosalind. 'No better place could have been selected for the performance than Lord Iveagh's beautiful gardens', declared the *Evening Herald*.[11] There were two evening performances and an afternoon matinee of *Twelfth Night*, all in aid of one of the dozens of charities helped by the Iveaghs, the Police-Aided Children's Clothing Society, which had been set up a few years earlier for the police to distribute shoes and clothes to destitute children they came across in the execution of their duties. This was perhaps one of the more esoteric of the many good causes which the Iveaghs espoused, although it doesn't quite win the prize. That must go to a motorists' lobby group, the Dust Prevention Committee, which campaigned against dusty roads.

6

ELVEDEN HALL

Suffolk

By the late 1880s Edward Cecil Guinness had three impressive addresses: Farmleigh, 80 St Stephen's Green and 5 Grosvenor Place in Belgravia, which he had leased from the Duke of Westminster in 1877. His wife Adelaide found the management of so many houses something of a strain, apparently: when Edward Cecil presented her with the deeds to a new house on Cowes as a birthday surprise, she burst into tears. Notwithstanding those tears, he now wanted a country estate in England, a place where he could entertain royalty on a royal scale. A chance remark by the Prince of Wales – 'You ought to buy some shooting in Norfolk' – prompted Edward Cecil to enquire after Elveden, a 17,000-acre estate straddling the borders of Norfolk and Suffolk.[1] At its heart lay one of the strangest, saddest country houses in England.

Elveden Hall belonged to Duleep Singh, the exiled Maharajah of the Sikh Empire. In 1863 the young Duleep, an avid sportsman, bought the estate and the rather ordinary Georgian mansion that went with it. The next year he married and, as his wife Bamba – a tragic figure, the illegitimate 15-year-old daughter of a German banker and an Ethiopian slave whom he found while she was teaching in an American mission school in Cairo – began to produce children, he decided that the old house wasn't big enough. John Norton, architect to the *nouveaux riches* and past president of the Architectural Association, was brought in to extend it and then to rebuild it in an unexciting Italianate style – on the outside at least. The interiors were a different matter entirely. Aided by photographs of Punjabi architecture and watercolours in the maharajah's collection, Norton and his team created a series of rooms which paid homage to Duleep Singh's Punjabi heritage, rooms filled with marble inlays and multifoil arches and sparkling mirror-glass ceilings, dripping with poppies and lotus flowers and irises.

Duleep Singh received a pension from the British government as

Right
An 1860s engraving of the original Georgian Elveden Hall, before Duleep Singh redesigned it.

Below
South front of the original Elveden Hall, photographed *ca.*1862. The figures in the garden are believed to include Duleep Singh's architect John Norton.

a small recompense for having his empire taken from him by the East India Company. But although the government advanced him nearly £200,000 for the purchase and remodelling of Elveden, it was an advance against this pension, and interest was payable on the loan. Duleep Singh insisted that he had been promised much more, and his sense of grievance grew, so that by the 1880s, and after an abortive attempt to regain his throne and a series of disastrous alliances with Russian agents and Irish republicans, he decamped to Paris with his mistress, a chambermaid called Ada. Elveden was dismantled and its contents sold at auction.

Above
Duleep Singh and his wife, the Maharani Bamba, about 1868.

The sale took place in 1886, and it was around this time that Edward Cecil began negotiations to buy the Elveden estate. But they did not go well. Edward rented nearby Riddlesworth Hall, described at the time as 'one of the best sporting estates in England', while Maurice de Hirsch, the German-Jewish financier and confidante of the Prince of Wales, laid siege to Duleep Singh in Paris, doing his best to persuade the maharajah to sell to Guinness so that Hirsch could then take Riddlesworth, which was usefully close to the Prince's Sandringham estate.[2] The negotiations dragged on for months, with Duleep Singh insisting he couldn't take a penny less than £250,000, before coming to an abrupt halt in June 1889 when the self-styled 'Sovereign of the Sikhs' wrote a peremptory note to Hirsch saying that the estate was no longer for sale. 'Please do not write to me on this subject again as my reply is final.'[3]

Undeterred, Edward Cecil continued his search for a seat. He heard that Tottenham House, an enormous early nineteenth-century mansion in the heart of Savernake Forest in Wiltshire, was coming up for sale, along with 40,000 acres. It belonged to the Brudenell-Bruces, marquesses of Ailesbury, and the reprobate 4th marquess, known as Willie, was up to his eyes in debt to moneylenders and desperate for ready cash. After some negotiations Sir Edward's offer of £750,000 was accepted, and he visited Tottenham and began to plan alterations to the house and grounds.

Unfortunately, he had reckoned without Willie's trustees, and in particular Willie's uncle, Sir Henry Brudenell-Bruce, who had a somewhat exaggerated sense of family honour. Sir Henry was outraged that 'a mere upstart merchant, a nouveau-riche Irishman', was trying to get his hands on the ancestral seat.[4] He fought for years to block his nephew's right to sell, taking the case right up the House of Lords, where a remarkably patient Sir Edward, who was raised to the peerage as Baron Iveagh of Iveagh in 1891, could only look on and await the outcome. He even had to hear Sir Henry claim in public that a Guinness representative had tried to bribe him with an offer of £50,000 if he withdrew his objections to the sale. By the spring of 1893 his patience was at an end; and he gave Willie's trustees an ultimatum: if the business wasn't settled by 1 May that year, he was withdrawing his offer. It wasn't, and he did.

And so five years after he began his search for an English country house, Edward Cecil, now Lord Iveagh, was no nearer to finding one. But luckily for him, if not for the last maharajah of the Sikh Empire, Duleep Singh died in Paris later that year; and the Elveden trustees swiftly approached Lord Iveagh with a view to reopening negotiations. On 3 April

Right
Elveden photographed in 1895, the year after Edward Cecil Guinness (now Lord Iveagh) bought it. The house now bore Duleep Singh's design.

1894 he signed an agreement to purchase, at a price of £160,000. The sale went through that July, and within weeks there were 150 men working on the site, cleaning the house, tidying the gardens and stables and installing a telephone office which connected to Thetford, the nearest town. Lord and Lady Iveagh moved into a farmhouse on the estate while the work was going on; and by Christmas 1894 they were hosting shooting parties, entertaining the wider Guinness clan and settling into their roles as responsible landowners by distributing beef, oranges and tea to their grateful tenants.

They entertained on a grand scale. At the end of 1895 the Duke of York, the future George V, came for a couple of days' shooting. Augustus Hare, that inveterate and indefatigable country house visitor, was in the house party, and revelled in the opulence. The house, he wrote at the time, 'is almost appallingly luxurious, such masses of orchids, [and] electric light everywhere'.[5] The quantity of game killed was 'almost incredible' (25,000 game were killed in the Iveaghs' first season, rising to a rather shocking 100,000 by 1900); but Hare, who did not shoot, was more impressed by the shooting luncheon parties, luxurious banquets 'with plate and flowers' set up in tents with boarded floors. The only jarring note, quite literally, was the electric player piano which the Iveaghs had set up in the house. According to Hare, 'it goes on pounding away by itself with a pertinacity which is perfectly distracting.'[6]

The Duke of York was back again in November 1896: 'I can't tell you how much I enjoyed those three splendid days shooting at Elveden,' he wrote to Iveagh; 'the best three days I have ever seen in England.'[7] The duke and duchess were regular guests, as were the duke's parents, the Prince and Princess of Wales. And perhaps because the Iveaghs felt that their house wasn't quite big enough or quite grand enough for entertaining royalty, they began to think of enlarging it.

Their choice of architect and contractor may have been influenced by one of their new neighbours in Suffolk. The Culford Hall estate, a few miles south of Elveden, belonged to the 5th Earl Cadogan, then Lord Lieutenant of Ireland and, like Iveagh, a staunch Unionist. In 1893 or thereabouts Cadogan had commissioned the Scottish architect William Young to transform Culford, creating a vast new entrance façade 260 ft long in an Italianate style, with a porte-cochère of Portland stone, and a new dining room wing. There was a tower, and the remaining façades of the old house were re-faced to harmonise with the new. The contractor for this work was the London firm of George Trollope & Sons.

Above
House party gathered at the transformed Elveden to mark the new century, 2 January 1900. The Prince of Wales, soon to become Edward VII, leans on his stick to the right of the doorway. Lord Iveagh is at far left; his son Ernest is at the back, while Rupert is at far right.

Young was a good architect, but not a great one. His main claim to fame was Glasgow's vast and opulent City Chambers (1881–90), although he also had a modest country house practice which besides Culford included the picturesque Tudor-Gothic Haseley Manor in Warwickshire (1875) and a remodelling of Gosford House, Lothian, for the 10th Earl of Wemyss (1891). But Iveagh obviously liked him: as we saw in Chapters 4 and 5, in 1896 he would design ballrooms for the Iveaghs at their house on St Stephen's Green and at Farmleigh on the edge of Phoenix Park.

Iveagh had commissioned Trollope & Sons to carry out the initial cosmetic tidying work when he took possession of Elveden; and he was evidently pleased with their work because when, in November 1899, Young signed contracts with Iveagh for a major remodelling of Elveden, the builder was Trollope & Sons again. The estimate for the work was £79,276. It was eventually exceeded by well over £30,000. Young died of pneumonia in 1900, aged only fifty-seven, with the scheme nowhere near completion; but his son Clyde, who took over his practice, completed the project to his father's designs.

That project was to double the size of Elveden, by building a replica (more or less) of the house that John Norton had built for Duleep Singh thirty years before to the east of the earlier building, and connecting the two with a centrepiece which consisted of a vaguely Adam-ish octagonal entrance hall behind which lurked a vast domed living hall. There was also a new servants' wing ranged around two courtyards, with more than thirty bedrooms for the domestic staff. There was separate accommodation in the house for the butler, the footman-in-waiting, the groom of the chambers, the under-butler, the housekeeper, the cook, Lord Iveagh's valet and visiting lady's maids.

Everything was on a massive scale. There was a new stable block, with coach houses and kitchens, and this, with a water tower and a collection of gardeners' and gamekeepers' cottages, looked more like a village than

Below
Drawing room in the west wing today, with interiors surviving from Duleep Singh's house.

Right
This photograph of the Moti Masjid – the 17th-century mosque built by Mughal emperor Aurangzeb within Delhi's Red Fort – is included in Lord Iveagh's 1890s photo album, perhaps provided by Caspar Purdon Clarke as one of several reference points for his Marble Hall at Elveden.

accommodation for Elveden's outdoor staff. Rooms in the new wing included a huge new dining room (the old one in Duleep Singh's wing was turned into a billiard room, and Bamba's boudoir became a smoking room), an oak-panelled room for Lord Iveagh and a Louis XVI morning room for his wife.

If this were all, Elveden would still be a great example of Edwardian eclecticism at its brightest. But the *pièce de résistance*, and in some ways the most puzzling feature in the new work, was that domed hall: in fact an Indian-style 'Marble Hall', 80 ft long and 45 ft high, and dripping with Hindu and Islamic motifs. Arcaded galleries at first-floor level rested on intricately carved pillars, multi-foil arches danced in the air, and a huge central dome decorated with floral motifs hovered over the entire space, like some exotic oriental version of St Paul's Cathedral. Built at a cost of some £70,000, it was described by Iveagh's biographer as an ostentatious millionaire's folly, yet praised by historian Clive Aslet as 'by far the most spectacular room of any Edwardian country house'.[8] Both statements are true.

What made Lord Iveagh opt for an Indian-style hall? The obvious answer is that it amused him to create some continuity with Duleep Singh's Rajput interiors, then barely twenty years old. But that is only half the

Above
The Marble Hall at Elveden today.

story. (And he painted over much of Duleep Singh's work in the original wing, which doesn't suggest an overly respectful attitude towards his predecessor.) More probable is that while the Marble Hall references the decorative scheme of the early 1870s, it is better seen as a fine example of a fashion for all things Indian which swept Britain towards the end of the nineteenth century: a fashion which found expression in the Durbar Room at Osborne House that the Lahore artist Bhai Ram Singh created for Queen Victoria in 1891; in the Indian billiard room which the same artist created for her son the Duke of Connaught's Bagshot Park in Surrey in the late 1880s; in the Colonial and Indian Exhibition which was opened by the Queen (who from 1876 was also Empress of India) in 1886, when the National Anthem was sung in Sanskrit.

The leading figure in the 1886 Exhibition, and the man who managed the Bagshot Park project, was Caspar Purdon Clarke, keeper of the India Museum at South Kensington (and later to be director of New York's

Below
The Durbar Room at Queen Victoria's Osborne House on the Isle of Wight.

Overleaf
Aerial view of Elveden Hall. To the right is Duleep Singh's house, remodelled by Lord Iveagh into his west wing. To the left is his east wing, which echoes the exterior (but not the interior) of the west. His domed Marble Hall is at the centre.

Metropolitan Museum); and it was Clarke who, with William Young, was responsible for Lord Iveagh's Marble Hall, working on a 1.5 percent commission. Inspiration came from various sources, notably the 1890 *Jeypore Portfolio of Architectural Details*, a pattern book of everything from copings and plinths to arches and balustrades and carved doors, prepared for the maharajah of Jaipur by Colonel S.S. Jacob, 'engineer to the Jeypore State'.[9] Clarke, who also advised Iveagh on more conventional furnishings in other parts of the house, maintained that the point of the Marble Hall was 'to reproduce, in England, the best examples of Moghul architecture'.[10] That was pushing things a little, in that he cheerfully mixed sources, some of them many hundreds of years apart. But however much Clarke – and perhaps Iveagh – thought that Elveden's Marble Hall was a textbook in marble to authentic Moghul architecture, it was what it was: a supremely confident homage to Imperialism, a guilty pleasure, a quintessentially Edwardian interior.

Opposite top
Lord Iveagh's guests at Elveden often posed for photographs on one of his new cars, as here in November 1902. Second from left at the front is the Prince of Wales, the future George V. Lord Iveagh is at back right. Adelaide is behind the prince.

Opposite bottom
King Edward VII, seated at centre, on one of his last shooting weekends at Elveden, January 1909. Among the grandees is the non-dancing Sir Frank Lascelles, standing third from left. Lord Iveagh is seated cross-legged at front right.

The new work took four years, and by the end Iveagh was getting rather tetchy and anxious about having his house back so that he could re-commence the round of house parties and shooting parties. 'We are greatly inconvenienced and upset by Trollopes' failing to finish the work in the dining room at Elveden,' he told his agent in September 1903. 'I really do not know what to do. We have a large shooting party coming to us before the end of this month and my wife will want quite 10 days before that time to furnish and arrange the room.'[11] The decoration still wasn't completed in October, when it became even more pressing, since the Prince of Wales was coming to stay for some shooting at the end of the month. And in December, the king himself would be there, the guest of honour at a large house party – thirty-two in all, including the Prime Minister, Arthur Balfour; Earl and Countess Cadogan; the Marquess and Marchioness of Londonderry; Earl and Countess Howe; and two of the Iveaghs' three boys, Rupert and Walter, with their wives. 'I do think it is too much when two people bring five servants,' muttered Lady Iveagh, after Lord and Lady Howe arrived with a valet, a maid, a secretary, a footman and a pony-boy.[12]

Did the hope of another title play some part in Lord Iveagh's purchase of Elveden? Perhaps, and if so, his plan worked. After his visit in December 1903, Edward VII urged Balfour to offer Iveagh something. 'He is well deserving of it,' said the king, 'and spends liberally of his colossal fortune on worthy and meritorious objects'.[13] The brewer was created Viscount Iveagh of Iveagh in December 1905. 'No one can be surprised,' gushed the *Tatler*. 'His hospitalities are princely and so are his public charities.'[14]

Elveden, wrote Iveagh's biographer, 'was the place where his happiest days were spent and where his hospitality was seen at its best'.[15] Both the king and the Prince of Wales were regular visitors, usually separately but sometimes together. (The king, who was an enthusiastic early adopter of the motor car, would drive over from Sandringham.) There were diplomats and politicians and aristocrats. The Duke of Wellington might be in the party. Alice Keppel, the king's mistress, certainly was: the king made sure of that. House-guests were entertained by the king's favourites M. Casano's orchestra, who played during afternoon tea and after dinner. Occasionally the Iveaghs hired the latest music hall turns. During the king's 1903 visit, for example, the famous Monsieur Inaudi, 'the lightning calculator from the London Hippodrome', was brought in to perform, along with the manager of the Hippodrome and Inaudi's own manager who acted as interpreter, since the lightning calculator couldn't speak English. His Majesty put Inaudi through his paces, giving him all kinds of problems to solve. What was the cube root of 389,017, he asked? '73', came back the answer almost instantly, despite the other guests rather unsportingly doing their best to put him off by shouting out other questions. Balfour tried to catch him out by asking for the fifth root of a large number, only to be told by Inaudi that the number wasn't to the fifth power. The king 'was very much amused'.[16]

Above
Monsieur Inaudi, the Lightning Calculator, 1903.

These house parties were surprisingly lively events. On one occasion Elizabeth, Countess of Fingall, a great friend of the Iveaghs with a country house of her own in County Meath, decided to dance an Irish jig in the Marble Hall, perhaps to keep warm – she reckoned that the hall was 'the coldest room in England'.[17] She called up to Casano, whose band was playing in the gallery, asking 'Can you play "The Rocky Road to Dublin"?' 'Never heard of it,' came down the reply. So she hummed it, and they picked up the tune. At this point, the countess decided she couldn't do a jig in her skirt – so she stripped to her petticoats and, because she had to have a partner, grabbed hold of Sir Frank Lascelles, the British ambassador to Berlin, and dragged him out onto the floor. Not having the faintest idea of how to dance a jig, the poor man stood there shuffling his feet while Casano's men improvised, she danced, and the king roared with laughter.

Countess Fingall was staying at Elveden in January 1910, when Edward VII paid his last visit to the Iveaghs. He was quite unwell and taking oxygen for his bad chest. Having given Lady Fingall a good telling-off over dinner for supporting women's suffrage – 'You women have enough power already! You can get all you want without the Vote' – he took her to one side in the drawing room afterwards and told her that he was very upset because one of her friends, a recent convert to spiritualism, had given him a message which was said to have come from his dead sister,

Princess Alice. The message was, 'The time is short. You must prepare.'

Did the friend give any proof that the message really was from Princess Alice, she asked?

'Yes,' he said. 'She said that I was to remember a day when we were on Ben Nevis together and found white heather and divided it.'[18]

Afterwards, the other guests teased the countess, assuming that the king had still been giving her a hard time over suffragettism. She didn't say anything, and she never saw the king again. He died four months later.

Below
Three generations at Elveden *ca.*1920. Lord Iveagh is in the middle of the back row, with his sons Rupert, to the right of him, and Ernest at the end of the middle row. Seated left are Rupert's wife Gwendolen and Ernest's wife Marie Clothilde. The girls in the front are Honor, Rupert's daughter, and Ernest's daughters Maureen, Oonagh and Aileen – the Guinness Golden girls. The boys are Walter's son Bryan and Rupert's son Arthur, Lord Elveden.

7

KENWOOD HOUSE

London

Opposite
Aerial view of Kenwood House.

Below
Edward Cecil Guinness, 1st Earl of Iveagh. Portrait by Henry Marriott Paget after Arthur Stockdale Cope, after 1912.

George V's birthday honours list for 1919 was a long one. So long, in fact, that although the first appointments were published on the king's birthday, 3 June, the last names didn't appear until August. Most of the nearly 10,000 individuals named were rewarded for their contributions to the war effort; but among the rear-admirals and the major-generals there were some less militaristic honours. The art dealer Joseph Duveen was given a knighthood for public services in connection with the extension of the Tate Gallery, which he had funded. Cecil Chubb was made a baronet, a reward for having presented Stonehenge to the nation the year before. And heading the list was Edward Cecil Guinness, now created the Earl of Iveagh and Viscount Elveden.

Edward Cecil was delighted. 'It is not possible for me adequately to express the feelings of gratefulness and loyalty to your Majesty which fill my heart,' he wrote to the king. 'I have done nothing to earn or deserve such a reward.'[1] That was stretching things a little: Iveagh's philanthropy was a byword in London and Dublin, and his various benefactions – well over £250,000 to form the Guinness Housing Trust in London and the similar Iveagh Trust for workers' housing in Dublin, half a million to scientific research, to name a few – were common knowledge in British and Irish society.

He was also well provided with palatial houses, although now he lived in them without Adelaide, who had died in 1916. He still

Left and below
Iveagh Trust workers' housing in Dublin, completed in 1901.

had the lease on 5 Grosvenor Place, which had become his main residence; and in Dublin there was 80 St Stephen's Green, and Farmleigh, where he usually entertained a large house party for the Dublin Horse Show. He regularly entertained George V and the Prince of Wales at Elveden; and, although he didn't spend much time at Ashford Castle, he also listed it as one of his seats in Debrett's. At the end of the nineteenth century, he bought the lease of the early Georgian Heath House in Hampstead, reckoned to be the highest house in London. (Its ground floor was higher than the cross on the dome of St Paul's.) And he kept a house on the Isle of Wight, where he entertained lavishly during Cowes Week, if he wasn't staying aboard his 120 ft-long racing schooner, the *Cetonia*.

You might think that was enough for anyone, no matter how wealthy they were. But the newly created Earl of Iveagh had one more house to buy. And in many ways, it was the most remarkable of them all.

Kenwood, also known as Ken Wood, was a modest country house on the edge of Hampstead Heath, belonging to the earls of Mansfield. The first earl, a distinguished Scottish lawyer who became Lord Chief Justice in 1756, celebrated his success by commissioning Robert Adam to remodel the existing early eighteenth-century house; and between 1764 and 1774 Adam added the spectacular Great Room. He also redecorated most of the other rooms and built a giant pedimented portico for the entrance front. Mansfield's nephew, who succeeded as the second earl in 1793, brought in Humphry Repton to landscape the grounds.

The Mansfields lived at Kenwood until 1910 when the 6th Earl, who preferred the family's Scottish seat of Scone Palace in Perthshire, let the house furnished to Grand Duke Michael of Russia, cousin to Tsar Nicholas II. A *Country Life* article from 1913 showed the house at its elegant Georgian best, full of Adam furniture and Mansfield family portraits.

Below
Portrait of William Murray, 1st Earl of Mansfield by John Singleton Copley, exhibited 1873.

But by then Earl Mansfield had already decided to sell and was exploring options for handing the house and its 200-acre estate to a building syndicate for development. A group of local residents led by the Liberal politician Sir Arthur Crosfield tried and failed to match Lord Mansfield's selling price of £550,000 and, although after the war as the Kenwood Preservation Council they managed to acquire 132 acres or so, and vest them in the London County Council as a public space, there were still fears that the remaining 76 acres would be built over and the house demolished, a fate that increasing numbers of country houses faced after the First World War. Those fears were heightened in September 1922 when a notice appeared in the press announcing that a local firm of auctioneers had received instructions to sell 'the whole of the remaining choice and valuable furnishings' at Kenwood.[2] The four-day sale, which began on 6 November, saw over a thousand lots leave the house: paintings by Turner, Watteau and Correggio; Adam furnishings and Louis XV furniture; Worcester and Dresden china; ormolu ornaments and antique glass. Some of the best pieces had already been carried off to Scone, but everything else was sold, leaving Kenwood bare from basement to attic.

Lord Iveagh knew Kenwood well, and he had direct experience of insensitive development in the neighbourhood. In the early 1900s the Hampstead mansion that he leased, Heath House, had been the subject of a battle with the Charing Cross, Euston and Hampstead Railway Company, which tried unsuccessfully to acquire it. It wasn't surprising that he should choose to support the campaign to save Kenwood.

Below
Kenwood House, south façade.

Above
The impressive Great Room at Kenwood House, designed by Robert Adam.

But he did rather more than support it. On 6 December 1924 Sir Arthur Crosfield wrote to the *The Times*, announcing that 'although I am not at liberty to say more at the present time, it can now be definitely stated that not a yard of the remaining 76 acres of Ken Wood will ever be sacrificed to the builders.'[3] Three months later the news broke: Lord Iveagh had bought the mansion and those 76 acres from the Earl of Mansfield for £107,900, and handed them over to trustees, who leased this surviving portion of the estate back to him. The plan was to make it available to the public either in ten years' time, or at Iveagh's death, whichever came first. *Country Life* applauded his generosity, relieved that 'this fine Adam house will be in the possession of one who can maintain it with suitable elegance'; and excited that Iveagh's pictures – 'one of the best private collections in the country' – might hang there.[4]

From the early days of their marriage, the Iveaghs had bought the occasional piece of tapestry or a painting, a fine carpet or a good piece of furniture, keeping them at Farmleigh, the St Stephen's Green house and 5

Grosvenor Place. The seventeenth-century Italian hangings in the dining room at Farmleigh, and an early Rembrandt of *Judas Returning the Thirty Pieces of Silver*, both bought in 1874, are good examples. They bought statues and antique cabinets in Florence; furniture and embroideries in Madrid; paintings in London. The first time they visited Duveen's famous Oxford Street gallery, Adelaide asked to see some screens; and as Joseph Joel Duveen showed the couple one after another, they – or rather Adelaide – said she would have them. Eventually Joseph Joel whispered to his son Joseph to find out who these high-spending new customers were. He nipped out of the shop, asked the Iveaghs' coachman and came back in, passing their name across to his father on a slip of paper, just as Adelaide was saying, 'You may think it strange, Mr Duveen, that I am buying so many screens.' 'Not at all, Lady Guinness,' said Joseph Joel. 'You have many fine homes.' She was delighted at being recognised, saying to her husband, 'You see, Edward. Mr Duveen knows who we are.' Years later, when Joseph Duveen told the story to one of Iveagh's sons, the man replied that 'At last I know why we had such a bloody lot of screens in the house!'[5]

Edward Cecil and Adelaide began collecting paintings in earnest in June 1887, the year after Guinness Breweries became a public company and Iveagh, then Sir Edward Guinness, retired from the direct management with a personal fortune of more than £6 million, while

Left
The spectacular ceiling of Robert Adam's Great Room.

Above
Poster for the 'Save Kenwood' campaign, by Poy (Pearcy Hutton Fearon), 1921.

remaining as chairman. The story goes that he walked into a Bond Street gallery one day in June 1887 and asked to see some fine pictures. The partners were out at lunch and the clerk refused, telling him he would have to wait until they came back. He turned on his heel, walked out, and tried his luck at the next dealer's gallery he came to, which was Thomas Agnew & Sons. William Agnew, one of the partners, was more attentive. When Iveagh (as I'm going to call him for simplicity's sake) announced that he wanted to start a collection of pictures, and said, 'I shall be glad if you will put before me anything good,' Agnew obliged with two paintings, *The Flower Gatherers* by François Boucher, and Aelbert Cuyp's *View of Dordrecht*. Lord Iveagh bought them both, paying £1,155 for the Boucher and £3,850 for the Cuyp. Three weeks later he was back with William Agnew, buying two paintings by Joshua Reynolds, including an unusual self-portrait of the artist wearing spectacles. A week later Agnew sold him another Reynolds and a Romney.

Over the next four years, Iveagh spent around half a million pounds with Agnew's, filling the Grosvenor Place mansion with more than 200 paintings. Friend and fellow collector J. Pierpont Morgan was apparently once heard to complain that there was never any point in calling in at Agnew's since 'anything they had that was worthwhile was always earmarked for Guinness'.[6] And Joseph Duveen was furious that while the Iveaghs might spend hundreds, or even thousands, with his gallery, he was spending hundreds of thousands at Agnew's: 'It makes me sick at my stomach to see people like Lord Iveagh buying mere art objects from us and paintings elsewhere,' he confessed.[7]

Agnew's supplied works by Rubens and Van Dyck, Watteau and Veronese, Gainsborough and Angelica Kauffman. Most came through private sales, with Agnew's taking 10 percent (their commission on auction sales was 5 percent). The largest single sum Iveagh paid was £27,500 in July 1888, for two Rembrandts and another Cuyp, being sold from the

Above
The dining room at Kenwood displaying Lord Iveagh's collection, including Rembrandt's *Portrait of the Artist* (1665–8).

Marquis of Lansdowne's collection at Bowood in Wiltshire. That was followed by £26,400 paid in December 1888 for portraits of Mrs Tollemache as Miranda and Lady Louisa Manners, both by Reynolds. All in all, Iveagh bought thirty-four Reynolds portraits. There were hardly any living artists in the collection: G.F. Watts's *Thetis*, purchased in 1890, was an exception. Otherwise, the nearest Iveagh came to acquiring contemporary art was six scenes by Sir Edwin Landseer, who had died in 1873; and he clearly didn't think much of them, since when he had his collection removed for safety from Grosvenor Place during the First World War, he left them hanging there.

Iveagh's spree lasted until 1891. Although he continued to buy, always through Agnew's, it was at a much slower rate: between December 1891 and 1908, when the relationship with Agnew's seems to have come to an end, he acquired just eighteen paintings, in contrast to the period from 1887 to 1891, when he was averaging a painting a week. The bulk of the collection remained at Grosvenor Place, and Iveagh often spent an hour alone with them in the picture gallery there. He refused to have them insured, saying that they were irreplaceable, and 'he did not need the money they had cost.'[8]

Below
The music room, with treasures from the Iveagh collection including Gainsborough's *Mary, Countess Howe* of 1764, on the far left.

By 1927, Lord Iveagh was seventy-nine years old and showing little sign of slowing down. In February he attended a dinner given by the Marquess of Salisbury for government supporters in the House of Lords. The following month he dined with the king and queen at Buckingham Palace; and in June he was at a Burlington House soirée given by the President of the Royal Academy, Sir Frank Dicksee, and then hosted a gathering

of 150 Conservative peers at Grosvenor Place. And he continued to support a bewildering range of charitable causes: £1,000 went towards the building of an Anglican church in New Delhi; another £1,000 to the National Playing Fields Association; £500 to support a new eye hospital in Westminster; a £500 donation to the fund for the Preservation of Ancient Cottages.

Apart from a brief visit to Elveden, Lord Iveagh spent the early summer in London, before making his customary visit to Dublin in August. Ernest, his middle son, and Ernest's three daughters, Aileen, Maureen and Oonagh, moved into his villa on the Isle of Wight for Cowes Week that year. Iveagh stayed at Farmleigh, where he had W.T. Cosgrave, head of the Irish Free State, and his wife to tea. Amused by the security arrangements for the visit – a motorcycle escort, armed guards lurking in the shrubbery – he pointed out to Cosgrave that the last time he had seen the nationalist leader with a police escort was in London, when he was under arrest.

While he was in Dublin, Iveagh went into the brewery most days, meeting with his fellow directors and holding court in the Chairman's room at St James's Gate. But at the end of the month, he was back at 5 Grosvenor Place and suffering from phlebitis; and his doctors ordered him to bed. There was no immediate cause for concern, but on 5 October he sent for Rupert, his eldest son, and told him that he had decided to resign as chair of Guinness Breweries and wanted Rupert to take his place. Two days later he was dead.*

Lord Iveagh was buried at Elveden after a private family service. 'Abide With Me' was sung at the graveside. There was a simultaneous memorial service in St Margaret's Westminster, with the king, the queen and Prime Minister Stanley Baldwin all sending representatives. The Conservative Party Conference, which was being attended by both Rupert and his brother Walter when their father's death was announced, observed two minutes' silence. *The Times* praised Lord Iveagh's 'cultured graciousness, his pleasant friendliness, his kindly sympathy'.[9] 'One of the greatest benefactors that Dublin ever had,' said the *Belfast Newsletter*.[10] He would be remembered, declared the *Irish Independent*, 'as one who used his great wealth, not in selfish pleasures, but in forwarding the public good'.[11]

* According to Iveagh's biographer, almost his last act was to draft a letter of dismissal to one of the brewery staff.

That great wealth amounted to around £14 million, making Iveagh one of the richest men in Britain, if not *the* richest. Exactly how he used it to forward the public good in relation to Kenwood only became clear after his death. In a codicil added to his will in December 1926, he said that it was 'my hope and desire that Kenwood House may be used permanently as an art gallery for the exhibition of pictures, tapestries, furniture and the like, open to and for the benefit of the public.'[12] Not only was he handing over the house and grounds to the public – and, incidentally, providing a legacy of £50,000 to be invested for their maintenance and upkeep – he was also bequeathing sixty-odd pictures, the pick of his collection, to hang on the walls. There were Rembrandts and Gainsboroughs, portraits by Van Dyck and seascapes by Van de Velde, no fewer than fourteen pictures by Sir Joshua Reynolds. The Boucher and the Cuyp which had begun his collection at Agnew's back in 1887 were included. There were Guardis of the Grand Canal in Venice; a Romney of Lady Hamilton; and if the bequest included a couple of Landseers, no one really minded.

Iveagh left detailed instructions as to how Kenwood should be managed. The trustees were his three sons, Rupert, Ernest and Walter; his private secretary C.H. Bland; the director of the National Gallery, Sir Charles Holmes (who supervised the picture hang); and a representative from London County Council. The trustees were allowed to charge for admission on two days a week at their discretion, so long as one of those days was not Sunday. And without actually being under any legal obligation, the council was urged to comply with Iveagh's wishes 'that the atmosphere of a gentleman's private park should be preserved', which meant no cricket, football, hockey, golf, baseball, real tennis, lawn tennis, badminton, croquet, bowls or any other game requiring 'the use of a special apparatus or instruments of play'.[13] Likewise, the trustees were asked to respect his wishes that the mansion itself 'should be preserved as a fine example of the artistic home of a gentleman of the eighteenth century'.[14]

That was not so easy. Most of Iveagh's finest furniture remained at Elveden or St Stephen's Green, or Grosvenor Place. The collection at Kenwood, such as it was, consisted mainly of over-restored Irish Georgian pieces or Edwardian reproductions. Nevertheless, the trustees did their best to present the mansion as a 'gentleman's house' – or rather, as Lord and Lady Iveagh's house, notwithstanding the fact that Adelaide had been dead for nine years when her husband acquired Kenwood, and he had only ever spent five nights in the place. One upstairs bedroom was furnished and described to the public as 'Her Ladyship's Bedroom'; another was 'The Earl of Iveagh's Bedroom'; its adjoining bathroom contained a bath which, according to legend, was never actually plumbed in.

But it was the paintings that captured the public's imagination, the Old Masters, the examples of French Rococo and above all, the eighteenth-century British portraits, all brought together not according to any academic criteria but simply because their owner liked them. While the mansion was being redecorated – by the same firm which sold off the Mansfield contents back in 1922 – the pictures went on tour, first to the Royal Academy and then to Manchester City Art Gallery.

On Thursday, 18 July 1928, Edward Cecil's eldest son Rupert Guinness, now the 2nd Earl of Iveagh, stood on the steps of the mansion and in a brief ceremony said how glad he was that London people were to have free enjoyment of 'one of the most magnificent specimens of a country palace' in the whole of England.[15] His brothers Ernest and Walter stood beside him, along with their wives and assorted Guinness children. The next day Kenwood opened to the public, and the public flocked to it – more than 12,000 in its first five days. They may not have seen the artistic home of a gentleman of the eighteenth century, or even the home of an Edwardian brewer. But what they did see was an unrivalled monument to public-spirited generosity. A monument to a good man.

Opposite
Johannes Vermeer's *The Guitar Player* (*ca.* 1672), one of Lord Iveagh's most significant purchases.

8

BIDDESDEN HOUSE

Wiltshire

By the time of the 1st Earl of Iveagh's death in 1927, his three sons all had country houses of their own. Rupert, who inherited the title, had married a daughter of the Earl of Onslow and built himself a new house at Pyrford Court, near the Onslow family seat of Clandon Park in Surrey. At his father's death he also had Elveden, Farmleigh and the big mansion on St Stephen's Green in Dublin.

In 1884, the 1st Earl had bought Knockmaroon, an estate close to Farmleigh, and in 1904 he gave it to his youngest son Walter on the latter's marriage. Around the same time the earl's second son, Ernest, bought some land across the road from Knockmaroon and employed

Below
The brothers Rupert, Ernest and Walter Guinness outside Farmleigh, probably in the late 1890s.

Opposite
Biddesden, the enchanting house bought by young newly-weds Bryan and Diana Guinness in 1931.

the architect Laurence Aloysius McDonnell, who had worked in the office of James Franklin Fuller, to build him another house, Glenmaroon, in a heavy Arts and Crafts style.

In 1911 Ernest added what was one of the first domestic indoor swimming pools in Ireland. (Glenmaroon was also equipped with a button attached to a coal scuttle, of all things: when it was pressed, an organ rose up through the floor and played *Cherry Ripe*, something which must have disconcerted visitors.) The two buildings, Knockmaroon and Glenmaroon, were linked via a pedestrian bridge over the road, and eventually came to be known simply as Glenmaroon.

Ernest also had Ashford Castle, left to him by the Ardilauns. And in 1921 he bought the *Belem*, a 167 ft-long schooner which had belonged to the Duke of Westminster. He renamed her the *Fantôme II* and took her on a round-the-world voyage with his three very eligible daughters, Aileen, Maureen and Oonagh, nicknamed by the press the Guinness Golden Girls.

Left
The impressive entrance hall at Glenmaroon, with wood-panelling, parquet flooring and a decorative ceiling.

Above
Bryan and Diana Guinness in Hyde Park in 1930, with their immense Irish wolfhound.

Although Walter had Knockmaroon, he and his wife Evelyn were soon to embark on a wonderfully romantic (and delightfully odd) project on the Sussex coast. Bailffscourt, the large country house they built between 1931 and 1935, was designed by Amyas Phillips, an antique dealer and, to quote the Grade II* listing entry for the house, 'an antiquarian rather than [an] architect'.[1] It was constructed almost entirely from salvaged historic materials. A window came from a derelict building near Muchelney Abbey in Somerset; the fifteenth-century oak door to the hall originally opened into a little medieval church in Hampshire; the entrance arch once graced a priory in Dorset; stone fireplaces and arches found their way to Bailiffscourt from demolition sites all over the country.

As work on Walter Guinness's antiquarian fantasy at Bailiffscourt got under way in the early 1930s, Walter's eldest son, Bryan, was searching for a country house of his own. He had married Diana, one of the six Mitford sisters, in 1929, when he was twenty-four and she was eighteen, and to begin with the young couple divided their time between a town house in Westminster and Pool Place, a smallish house on the Sussex coast belonging to Bryan's parents and close to Bailiffscourt. Both archetypal Bright Young Things, they led a hectic social life in London, mixing with artists and writers like Augustus John and Henry Lamb and Evelyn Waugh

Above
Diana Freeman Mitford's wedding day, 1929. Her bridesmaids included sisters Nancy and Unity; the younger Debo and Jessica were absent due to illness.

(who dedicated his 1931 novel, *Vile Bodies*, 'with love to Bryan and Diana Guinness'). Bryan also had literary aspirations of his own: his first collection of verse, *Twenty-Three Poems*, appeared in 1931 to polite, rather than rapturous, applause. 'Mr Guinness's faults as a poet will soon be cured,' declared the *Liverpool Daily Post*. 'They are the result of youth.'[2]

Walter Guinness, a prominent Conservative politician who was raised to the peerage as Baron Moyne in 1931, seems to have found living next door to his ultra-sociable daughter-in-law rather a strain. A year after their marriage he offered to buy the newly-weds a place in the country of their own – perhaps, Bryan speculated later, because Diana talked loudly of building an observation tower of glass and steel beside Amyas Phillips's homage to the past. When Bryan said he and Diana loved being at Pool Place, and could think of nowhere else they would like to live, his father pointedly suggested that 'it was not a good plan for families to live on top of each other'.[3]

They eventually took the hint and began searching around for a modest country house which was a suitably long distance from Bryan's parents. Almost at once they found Biddesden, on the border of Wiltshire and Hampshire. It was a stunningly beautiful sixteen-bedroom Queen

Anne house of the softest red brick with stone details; and it also boasted electric light, radiators, telephones and garaging for four cars. They went to tea with the owner, a Mrs Fothergill, who took to them straight away, and they fell in love with the house. But Mrs Fothergill's asking price was twice what Bryan's father had offered them; and so they kept looking.

There was Boyton Manor, a lovely Jacobean mansion in the Wylye Valley in Wiltshire; but Diana 'felt it out of tune with her more Palladian taste'.[4] They looked at Ashdown, high on the Berkshire Downs, an exquisite little Dutch dolls' house built by Earl Craven in the early 1660s as a country retreat, so the story went, for Elizabeth of Bohemia, the 'Queen of Hearts'. But Ashdown was only being offered on a short lease, and they wanted somewhere where they could settle down.

With a pocketful of agents' particulars, Bryan and Diana were still house hunting a year later, when they happened to pass Biddesden again. Remembering how lovely it was, and full of youthful optimism, they instructed their agent to offer half the asking price. To their delight Mrs Fothergill remembered them from their earlier visit and agreed to accept it.

The architect of Biddesden is not known, but his client most definitely is. General John Richmond Webb was the local MP, and a distinguished army officer who served in the War of the Spanish Succession, was seriously wounded at the Battle of Malplaquet in 1709 and was made commander-in-chief of all land forces in England three years later. He began Biddesden in about 1711, shortly before the death of his first wife Henrietta Borlase, with whom he had seven children. In 1720, four years before his own death at the age of fifty-six, he married his wife's widowed sister Anne, who had been living with him for some time and who bore him three more.

Whoever designed Biddesden – and Webb himself has been suggested, although it is hard to see on what grounds – they showed an original grasp of domestic architecture. The exterior is all curves, from the row of three circular ox-eye windows above the front door to the round-headed sashes that light both the main floors, the segmental-headed windows to the attic storey and the segmental pediment that breaks out from the entrance façade. The new house displayed souvenirs of Webb's military career: martial trophies perched above the entrance; a curious Vanbrughian crenellated round tower rose from the north-east corner of the house and was apparently built to house a church bell which the general looted after the fall of Lille in 1708.

Above left
The hall at Biddesden with John Wootton's massive portrait of General Webb of 1712.

Above right
Diana Guinness with young sons Desmond and Jonathan, photographed by Yevonde.

Most remarkable of all was the sight which greeted visitors to Biddesden as they came into the two-storey entrance hall – a colossal equestrian portrait of Webb painted by John Wootton in 1712. This fitted so perfectly between panelling and cornice at the far end of the hall that it was hard to tell if it was painted to fit the house, or if the house was designed to fit the painting.

The Wootton portrait went with Biddesden. Mrs Fothergill told Bryan and Diana that it was included in the sale, and that there was a legend that if it were ever taken down, the general would come back to haunt the owner, riding his ghostly horse up and down the staircase. They didn't believe her. But they didn't move the painting, either.

The couple moved into Biddesden in 1931. A son, Jonathan, had been born in March 1930, and Diana was already pregnant again: her second child, Desmond, was born that September. The Guinnesses didn't make too many drastic changes to the interior of the house, which was in any case modest and quietly appealing in its early Georgian simplicity. The fashionable interior decorator Dolly Mann was brought in to advise on new paint schemes for the main rooms, all soft neo-Georgian greys and pinks and greens; and several internal walls were taken out to give more space. Three rooms on the west side of the house were thrown together to make a long drawing room, for example, with pale dove-grey panelling; the main bedroom was formed from two smaller bedrooms, and given a Syrie Maugham-like treatment of whites and off-whites, presumably by Dolly Mann. Another bedroom in the south-east corner of the house retained a curious brass locking device: a horizontal bar which could be raised by yanking on a cord next to the bed. It is not clear whether this was intended to keep out potential suitors or to let them in without having to go to the trouble of getting out of bed.

In the grounds, Bryan commissioned the Bloomsbury Group sculptor Stephen Tomlin to create a lead figure of a woman for the walled garden. But the most significant architectural addition came from the artist and architect George Kennedy, who designed a domed gazebo-cum-bathing pavilion on the edge of the garden, with a reflecting pool that

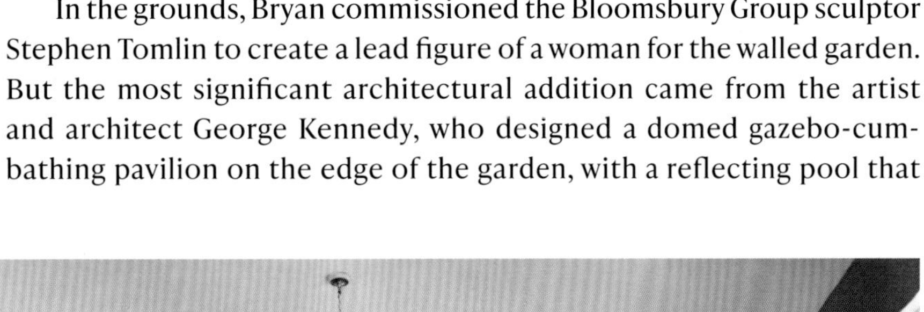

Below
The living room at Biddesden as featured in *Country Life*, 1938.

was deep enough for swimming. The pavilion, described rather cautiously by Christopher Hussey in 1938 as 'an unusual and attractive design in flint and brick', was another concoction of curves, topped with a copper cupola and equipped with an ingenious system for removing weeds and other detritus.[5] Kennedy provided 'scum channels' in the sides of the pool, a little above the normal water level and connected to a drain. A cistern in one corner of the pavilion could be flushed every now and then, causing the water level in the pool to rise suddenly and the weed to be carried away into the channel and out into the drain. Perhaps more interesting than the drains were the mosaics of three muses which decorated the pavilion: executed several years after it was finished, they were the work of the brilliant Russian-born mosaicist Boris Anrep, whose work brightened the floors of the Bank of England, Westminster Cathedral and, most famously, the National Gallery (where he depicted Diana Guinness as Polyhymnia, the Greek muse of poetry and dance).

Above
The bathing pavilion, designed by George Kennedy.

Diana loved a party, and much of the Guinnesses' time at Biddesden was spent entertaining. Guests included Aldous Huxley, Augustus John and Evelyn Waugh. The painter Henry Lamb and his wife Pansy lived nearby: Lamb painted a group portrait of Bryan, Diana and their first son Jonathan. John Betjeman was a good friend of Bryan's from their Oxford

Right
Boris Anrep's mosaics inside the bathing pavilion.

days, and he spent almost every other weekend at the house. He used to lead the Biddesden house guests in singing hymns after dinner, for which act of piety he was once rewarded with a nightmare, in which he was handed a mourning card engraved with his name and a date, which he was convinced was the date of his own death. When Penelope Chetwode broke off her engagement to Betjeman and fled to the south of France in 1933, the jilted lover took refuge at Biddesden while his host wrote a passionate but unhelpful letter to Penelope, telling her that if she had finished the affair because of parental pressure, 'I cannot sufficiently express how much I deprecate your cowardice.' And if she had put off Betjeman simply because she wanted to travel, as she claimed, 'I would

Above
The east front of the house, Roland Pym's *trompe l'oeils* just visible.

not have believed it possible that the shallowest nature could have urged so basely selfish and mundane an excuse.'[6] Not surprisingly, the letter didn't improve matters: only after Betjeman took Nancy Mitford's advice to go after her and get her were the couple reconciled. They married that summer.

For some years, the critic Lytton Strachey, his lover Ralph Partridge and Partridge's wife, the artist Dora Carrington (who was in love with Strachey) had been living close by at Ham Spray House, a lovely Regency villa bought in 1924; and by the time the Guinnesses moved to Biddesden the trio had been joined by Frances Marshall, who was in love with Partridge. Strachey and Carrington were 'my dearest and most welcome guests,' recalled Diana.[7] While she was in London for the birth of Desmond, as a welcome-home surprise, Carrington painted a delightful *trompe-l'oeil* figure in a blind window on the west front of Biddesden, a girl seated at a table peeling an apple while her cat looked on. The cat was modelled on Strachey's cat, Tiberius.

After Strachey died of cancer in January 1932, the Guinnesses did their best to comfort a distraught and grieving Carrington, taking her riding and organising picnics and other outings. It was no use: two months after Strachey's death she came over to Biddesden and asked to borrow Bryan's gun, saying she wanted it to shoot rabbits. Instead, she took it back to Ham Spray and shot herself with it.

Various members of the Mitford clan were frequent visitors to Biddesden. Carrington described a luncheon party with Diana's mother, Lady Redesdale, 'very sensible and no upper class graces' – and the younger sisters. Debo 'completely won me by her high spirits and charm', while 16-year-old Unity, who was to fall in love with Hitler and attempt suicide in Munich when war broke out, was 'very marvellous and grecian'.[8] Diana's older sister Pamela moved in next door and managed the 200-acre farm that came with the Biddesden estate.

But soon after Pamela moved in, Diana moved out. In the spring of 1932, at a dinner party to celebrate a friend's birthday, she met the politician Sir Oswald Mosley, who was preparing to re-launch his recently formed New Party as the British Union of Fascists. They began an affair; and the following year Bryan gave Diana a divorce, providing her with the usual grounds, adultery 'at an hotel in Brighton'.[9]

In September 1936 Bryan married again. His bride was Elisabeth Nelson, the daughter of publisher (and Scottish international rugby player) Thomas Nelson. The marriage was a happy one, and the couple

Above
The *trompe l'oeil* windows. On the left is Dora Carrington's original on the west front, showing a cat, a canary in a cage and a girl peeling an apple. The other three were created later by Roland Pym on the east front.

had four sons and five daughters. They continued to live at Biddesden, and Bryan – who became the 2nd Lord Moyne in 1944, when his father was killed in Cairo by terrorists – turned into an enthusiastic farmer, while producing a steady stream of gentle poems, plays and novels.

His output included a charming children's book, *The Story of Johnny and Jemima* (1936), which was based on tales his mother used to tell him as a child. It was illustrated by the painter and theatre designer Roland Pym and marked the beginning of a long friendship and collaboration between the two men. Pym illustrated several more of Bryan's books, and another by Bryan and his youngest daughter Mirabel Guinness, *Biddesden Cookery*, a collection of recipes gathered by the family and their staff over the years. But Pym's most delightful contribution to Biddesden was a group of three *trompe-l'oeils* in the blind windows on the east front. Obviously inspired by Carrington's earlier figure of a girl and a cat on the west front, they step right out of a Jane Austen novel. In one, a girl who could be *Mansfield Park*'s Mary Crawford plays the harp; in another, a Regency buck, a Darcy or a Mr Knightley, surprises another girl at her needlework, with what looks like a declaration of love; and in the third, two girls who might be Bennet sisters pore over a letter. All are painted slightly smaller than life-size, to accentuate the fantasy that we're looking in at them on the other side of the painted glazing bars of the non-existent windows. One can't help wondering if there is a thread connecting the three scenes, a narrative that remains tantalisingly out of reach.

Below
Pym's illustration of the house from *Biddesden Cookery*.

And that is the point. Pym encourages us to engage with his creations, to make up our own stories, to take these admittedly slight scenes and give them a life beyond themselves. They charm, they intrigue; and in their simple whimsicality they help to make Biddesden the most quietly attractive of all the Guinness family's country houses.

9

LUTTRELLSTOWN CASTLE

County Dublin

Aileen Guinness, granddaughter of the 1st Earl of Iveagh, was the oldest of Ernest Guinness's daughters, and the first of the three fabled 'Guinness Golden Girls' to find a husband and a country house.

Opposite
Luttrellstown Castle, a wedding present from Ernest Guinness to his eldest daughter Aileen.

Below
Aileen Guinness, who married Brinsley Sheridan Plunket in 1927.

On 16 November 1927 she walked down the aisle of St Margaret's Westminster in a medieval dress of ivory-white velvet, beaded with pearl and diamanté embroidery and hauling a velvet train lined with gold lamé, to be wed to Brinsley Sheridan Plunket, son of the 5th Lord Plunket, and a second cousin: his grandmother was Anne, the daughter of Benjamin Lee Guinness. Aileen was twenty-three, and Brinsley was one year older. It has always been said that Luttrellstown Castle, a few miles west of Ernest's Glenmaroon and Lord Iveagh's Farmleigh, was a wedding present to Aileen from a doting father. She recalled in later life that as a young girl she used to ride over from Glenmaroon to admire the castle, and one day she sat on a nearby wishing seat and wished that she would live there someday. 'You can't imagine my joy and surprise when my father made me a present of the Castle,' she said.[1] On the other hand, she also sometimes gave a mischievous (and apparently groundless) alternative version of events, claiming that the wedding present story was 'nonsense – I bought it myself, without him knowing.'[2]

Luttrellstown was a vast jumble of towers and courtyards, added to at various periods

in a complicated building history which dates back to the Middle Ages. But it was basically a nice example of late Georgian Gothick Revival, extended and remodelled at the end of the eighteenth century for Henry Luttrell, 2nd Earl of Carhampton. Various names have been put forward as likely architects for the work, including Sir Richard Morrison, the great exponent of Picturesque castle-building in Ireland; and the artist and architect Thomas Sandby, who worked for the Earl of Carhampton's brother.

The Luttrells, who held the estate for six centuries, were not popular. In fact, their bad habit of betraying friends, causes and family members made them the most hated family in Ireland, according to some accounts. The 2nd Earl's zeal in putting down the 1798 rebellion, and the hostility this provoked, may have led him to decamp to another of his seats, Cobham Park in Surrey; and the following year he sold Luttrellstown to Luke White, who started out as an itinerant bookseller in Belfast and rose to become a banker to the Irish government. (At one stage he lent the government one million pounds at 5 percent.) White laid out new pleasure grounds, extended a lake on the property and was probably responsible for a now lost hexagonal cottage orné, thatched and with walls of bark and a ceiling covered in shells.

Above
Henry Luttrell, 2nd Earl of Carhampton, one of the most hated men in 18th-century Ireland.

White's son was raised to the peerage as Baron Annaly in 1863, but the family tended to live on their English estates, and they sold the castle to a Major Hamilton in 1919. It was Hamilton's widow who sold Luttrellstown to Ernest Guinness.

Newly-weds Aileen and Brinsley seem to have spent time and money in modernising the house. An English landscape designer, Percy Cane, was brought over to design a formal garden; and by 1932 the house was said to have been 'entirely decorated and renovated in modern style, still keeping in harmony with the almost medieval characteristics', until it boasted 'one of the finest and most beautifully conceived interiors of any house in Ireland'.[3] The architect or decorator responsible for this work isn't known.

But the marriage was not happy. Aileen had an affair with Douglas Fairbanks Senior, while Plunket was addicted to some curious sexual practices which were not to Aileen's taste. ('She was forced to clean up after him', gossiped their incorrigible cousin by marriage Chips Channon: 'pink crepe de chine sheets too!'[4]). By 1939 Aileen was petitioning for divorce. She was granted a decree nisi in May 1940, and in the following year Plunket, who had joined the RAF as a flight-lieutenant, was killed in a dogfight over Sudan. Aileen went to America, and during the war Luttrellstown was the residence of the Italian ambassador, Vincenzo Berardis; a fawning profile of him in the *Irish Independent* praised his Fascist masters for the regeneration of Italy and described Luttrellstown (now a 'Castello') as 'the finest diplomatic residence in Ireland.'[5]

Aileen reclaimed Luttrellstown after the war and began the task of redecorating and refurnishing the house. Her partner in this was the brilliant and underrated English interior designer Felix Harbord. Born in Suffolk in 1906, Harbord had worked as Librarian and Art Keeper for

Below
A rustic arch in the grounds of Luttrellstown, constructed in about 1780.

the Bute Collection at Mount Stuart in the 1930s. During the Second World War he served in the Royal Engineers before being recruited as one of the twelve 'monuments men' who worked with SHAEF, Supreme Headquarters Allied Expeditionary Force, tracking down art objects looted by the Nazis. They were found in mines and brick kilns, in the tunnels of Berchtesgaden and in plain sight in German museums. Göring, said Harbord at the time, 'was the chief looter. He ... looted with great taste.'[6] In June 1945 Harbord discovered the contents of Berlin University Library, several thousand rare volumes, stored in wooden packing crates in a warehouse. Around the same time he also discovered a beautiful glass and ormolu chandelier, later claiming it was lying abandoned and damaged in a street in the North Rhine-Westphalian town of Kleve. He packed it in empty munition boxes and shipped it back to his former employer, Augusta Crichton-Stuart, who had it repaired and hung in the drawing room of Bute House in Edinburgh. Bute House was handed over to the state in 1966, eventually becoming the First Minister of Scotland's official residence. The chandelier still hangs there, the subject of occasional embarrassing questions about what a piece of Nazi loot of uncertain provenance is doing in the building.

Left
The ballroom, a collaboration between Aileen Plunket and the decorator Felix Harbord.

Above
The staircase: Harbord would move pictures and furniture from room to room as he found more interesting pieces.

Harbord's name first appeared in the Luttrellstown visitors' book in June 1946, and he stayed at the house sixty times over the next quarter of a century. He also worked for Aileen as a party decorator: in the summer of 1947 she gave a coming-out dance for her daughter Neelia at Harbord's Knightsbridge house; and three years later he created a spectacular Regency setting for her younger daughter Doon's *début*. The relationship between Aileen and her decorator was a wonderfully fruitful one, with Harbord transforming Luttrellstown's interiors into some of the finest post-war state rooms in Ireland.

The evolution of the house is hard to disentangle. Harbord bought in chimneypieces and carpets and paintings, gilded reliefs and tapestries found in London and Dublin, in little antique shops and country auctions. They might sit happily together for a while, until he found something else that suited a room better, when they would be moved to another space. Initially, for example, the staircase hall was given an almost Baroque chimneypiece, which was originally intended for the dining room, and new doorcases. Years later Harbord sourced a ceiling painting of a mythological scene, then thought to be by Sir James Thornhill but more recently reckoned to be by a continental artist and dated to around 1730; and this was installed in the staircase hall. When a set of hunting scenes was found for the ballroom, the historical portraits that hung there were moved into the staircase hall.

Below
The ballroom still retains many elements of Harbord's designs today.

His dining room was spectacular. The walls vibrate with trophies and festoons that seem to all intents and purposes to be Georgian: they were designed entirely by him. A painting of 1753 of the *Triumph of Bacchus and Ceres* fills the ceiling. The walls were a soft yellow, the carpet an Aubusson. Everywhere there was quality, but not a slavish adherence to period; the overall feel was light, witty, and Georgian, but not of any fixed date. There were English looking glasses, painted chairs said to come from the Château de Maintenon, a carpet from the Russian Imperial Manufactory. The aim of decorator and client seems to have been to suggest the eighteenth century, but not to live in it. And not to complete it. The process of making was the point. The journey was the thing, not the arriving. The results were whimsical and, frankly, a masterpiece of post-war country house decoration.

Unfortunately, Felix Harbord had a habit of sailing close to the wind. His discovery of the 'abandoned' chandelier in war-torn Kleve gave a hint of that. Then in 1960 he was hauled into the British Bankruptcy Court over an unpaid bill to a surveyor – 'a ridiculous oversight by a man in my employ', he loftily explained to the *Daily Express*.[7] And in 1972 his long working relationship with Aileen Plunket came to an abrupt end when Aileen sued him for the return of eight paintings, most of them seascapes by Sir Oswald Brierly which had once belonged to her grandfather, the 1st Earl of Iveagh. He contended she had told him to sell them; she maintained she hadn't. And the judge in the case, Justice Milmo, believed her, although he said he was satisfied that the decorator 'had no intention of pocketing the proceeds of the sale'.[8] Harbord was ordered to pay £1,400 to the Westminster dealer to whom he had sold the paintings (twice the price they gave for them) plus the costs of the four-day action, estimated at £1,000. Cecil Beaton, who was a client and a loyal friend of Harbord's, wrote Aileen a vitriolic letter after the case, telling her he hoped she would be happy alone and getting 'older and uglier'. He signed it 'Yours Never'.[9]

Aileen Plunket lived a peripatetic life, drifting between Ireland, England and America, a country she loved. She was there in 1940, when her divorce to Brinsley Plunket went through; and after the war she continued to make frequent trips to New York. It was at a party in Manhattan that she met the Yugoslav designer Valerian Stux-Rybar, reputed to be the

Overleaf
The Gothic hall: light, airy and delightfully playful.

world's most expensive interior decorator. In December 1956 the couple were married at Christ Church, not far from Stux-Rybar's Park Avenue apartment, an opulent concoction in which the walls were covered in red velvet, the floor was made of stainless steel and the living room was presided over by a carved bust of Ferdinando de Medici – made of crystal. His clients included Rothschilds, James Goldsmith and Christina Onassis. Fortunately for Luttrellstown, Stux-Rybar was content to leave his wife and Felix Harbord to their own devices at the castle. But the marriage didn't last. Stux-Rybar was, in Aileen's words, 'a mistake'. They divorced in 1965.

With and without a husband, Aileen was a consummate hostess, thriving on entertaining. Interviewed for a profile piece in the *Sunday*

Below
A page from Aileen's photograph album shows a house party at Luttrellstown over Christmas 1932.

Telegraph in 1983, she recalled swimming parties, fancy dress parties, drag parties (including one in which a female guest was smitten by a very attractive man, only to find out over dinner that he was a she). There were Floor parties, in which all the servants would be given the night off and everyone had to sit and eat on the floor; and Twist parties: 'I flew in this wonderful black American dance teacher from Paris to teach people how to twist,' she said. There were even Hippy parties: 'I just loved the hippy era, all those beads and "Are You Going to San Francisco".'[10]

After the little misunderstanding about Aileen's pictures, Harbord's connection with Luttrellstown Castle came to an end. He died in Paris in 1981. By then, Aileen was nearing eighty and living alone, except for a small army of servants. 'I do love it here,' she said, but 'it seems rather silly to continue on in such a large place.'[11] So in 1983 the house and its 570-acre estate were put up for sale, at an asking price of around £3.5 million; and over three days in September, Luttrellstown Castle's contents went under the hammer.

Highlights of the first day's sale, which realised over £1.5 million, were a pair of George II side-tables originally from Wardour Castle in Wiltshire, which went for £88,000; and a commode which once graced the Fontainebleau bedchamber of Louis XV, a fact which doubled its estimate after its provenance was confirmed and ensured that it went for £64,000. By the end of the third day, the sale had made £2.3 million, a record for an Irish country house sale. Dealers, curious neighbours and family members crowded into a huge marquee on the lawn, as one after another, the items gathered together so carefully by Aileen and Felix Harbord were sold. Through it all, wrote one poetically inclined reporter, 'Mrs Plunket's beautiful face stood out against the crowd like a cool water lily in a pond.'[12]

10
CLANDEBOYE HOUSE

County Down

Opposite
Clandeboye House.

Below
Maureen Guinness and Basil Hamilton-Temple-Blackwood on their wedding day, 3 July 1930.

Most of the Guinness family bought country houses. Few of them built one from scratch, although as we have already seen, plenty of them remodelled existing buildings, sometimes quite drastically. But only one Guinness married into an ancient house, both figuratively and literally. That was Maureen, the second of Ernest Guinness's three Golden Girls. When in July 1930 the 23-year-old Maureen – one of the most eligible women in London Society, according to the press – walked down the aisle of St Margaret's Westminster with her father, followed by eleven bridesmaids decked out in white tulle with gold head-dresses, and promised to love, honour and obey Basil Hamilton-Temple-Blackwood, heir to the Marquessate of Dufferin and Ava, she knew that one day the title and the Dufferins' ancestral seat of Clandeboye House in County Down would be his – and hers.

But she couldn't have known how soon that day would come. It was only nineteen days later, while the newly-weds were honeymooning in Italy, that they heard that Basil's father, the 3rd Marquess, had died in a plane crash on his way home from Le Touquet.

Clandeboye was a comfortable, unremarkable late-Georgian house, two-storeyed and grey with a columned portico on the entrance front and a big bow looking out onto the gardens, behind which lay a saloon, flanked by a drawing room and a

Above
The 1st Marquess of Dufferin and Ava.

Opposite
Helen's Tower, an act of filial piety.

dining room. Basil's grandfather, the 1st Marquess, who had a distinguished career as Governor-General of Canada and Viceroy of India, made several attempts to transform Clandeboye into something a little livelier. In the 1840s he asked the prolific Scottish architect William Burn to come up with a scheme for a fashionably neo-Elizabethan fantasy, but this came to nothing, and in 1865 the 1st Marquess turned to the Gothic Revival architect Benjamin Ferrey, who produced drawings for a Scotch Baronial remodelling, with steep dormers and corner turrets. That too was shelved, but the Marquess commissioned yet another romantic reinvention of Clandeboye, this time from the Belfast architect William Henry Lynn, who came up with plans in a style that Dufferin called 'Scotch Jacobean' but which actually looked like a cross between Balmoral and the French Renaissance, with a strong dash of Walter Scott – all conical roofs and battlements and romance.

Fortunately, perhaps, Lynn's scheme went the way of the others, and the 1st Marquess's most lasting architectural contribution to Clandeboye was Helen's Tower, a wonderfully romantic folly on a hilltop at the southern end of the estate, and about a mile from the main house. Designed by William Burn in 1848, but not completed until 1862, Helen's Tower became a tribute to Dufferin's mother Helen, granddaughter of the playwright Richard Brinsley Sheridan; although it may initially have been conceived as a Famine project, providing employment for estate workers and local communities. Burn's drawing, which shows the tower as it was built, is simply labelled 'Gamekeeper's tower Clandeboye 1848'.[1] When it was finished, the romantic Dufferin asked some of the leading poets of his day for verses to commemorate Helen and the tower, having them engraved and fixed on metal plates to the walls of a pretty octagonal panelled Gothic room at the top of the tower. It was a whim that survived Helen's death, from breast cancer, in 1867, and to the original poems by the likes of Tennyson and Carlyle were added verses by Browning, Kipling and others, dedicated to the marquess or his marchioness, Harriet Rowan Hamilton. Tennyson's contribution began:

Helen's Tower here I stand.
Dominant over sea and land.
Son's love built me, and I hold
Mother's love in lettered gold.[2]

By the time that Maureen Guinness came to Clandeboye as its new marchioness in 1930, Helen's Tower had become a destination for Belfast tourists, 'all charabancs and ginger beer', recalled Harold Nicolson, a cousin of the Dufferins on his mother's side.[3] In 1937 Nicolson published an affectionate life of the 1st Marquess, peppered with equally affectionate memories of childhood visits to Clandeboye. He remembered how, as he ascended the tower during one of his stays with his cousins, he went past the ground floor where the caretaker had his kitchen, 'and from which the smell of rabbit-stew and potato-cakes creeps into the upper chambers, mingling the living savour of an Irish bothy with the dead scent of closed rooms, of Victorian woodwork, of camphor and of decaying brocades'.[4]

After abandoning their Italian honeymoon to attend Basil's father's funeral at Clandeboye, the new marquess and marchioness stayed away from County Down for nearly a year, preferring to live in their Knightsbridge town house at Hans Place, which Maureen had bought in 1930 for £8,000. The couple didn't return to Clandeboye until August 1931, when they brought with them a new member of the family – their daughter Lady Caroline Blackwood, who had been born the previous month and who was baptised in the private chapel at Clandeboye, with water brought from the River Jordan. She wore the same white Carrickmacross lace dress in which her mother had been baptised twenty-four years before.

Traditional celebrations which had been planned to mark both Basil's coming of age in April 1930 and his marriage to Maureen that July had all been put on hold because of the death of the 3rd Marquess. Now the Dufferins made up for lost time, throwing a huge ball in the banqueting hall at Clandeboye for 350 of their tenants and estate workers to mark Lady Caroline's christening. It was decked out with flags and bunting for the occasion. There were speeches and presentations – the tenants gave the couple a pair of solid silver goblets, and the estate workers

Above
The octagonal Gothic room at the top of Helen's Tower, its panelling set with poems by Tennyson, Browning and others.

contributed a solid silver Celtic salver – and dancing went on into the early hours. Several members of the Guinness family were there, including Lord Elveden, son of the 2nd Earl of Iveagh, and his sister Honor. Maureen looked striking in a chiffon velvet frock of sapphire blue, and the press noted approvingly that both the marquess and the marchioness danced with tenants and employees. One of the house guests was the poet John Betjeman, an old friend of Basil's from their time at Oxford. Unsure about these quasi-feudal practices, and uncomfortable with the younger guests who would play their dance records in the library – 'too many smart, bright young people to suit me' – he felt very Bolshevistic and got tight.[5] Maureen took to her bed after the ball and stayed there for several weeks.

The Dufferins were back in London by the beginning of October, but that visit to Clandeboye was the first of many in the 1930s. All their children were christened in the private chapel there: a second daughter, Perdita, in October 1934; and a son and heir to the Dufferin titles and estates, Sheridan Frederick, four years later. They fell into the habit of hosting a big house-party at Christmas and another at Easter, and they usually took a party to the International Tourist Trophy motor-car race, which was held every year at the beginning of September on

Left
Maureen photographed with her daughter Caroline in 1934.

public roads in County Down until 1936, when a car skidded, left the road and ploughed into a group of spectators, killing eight and injuring twenty-three in what was then the worst accident in the history of motor racing.

Although the 1st Marquess's plans for a dramatic remodelling of Clandeboye had come to nothing, he had made some alterations to the house, creating a new entrance by converting a domestic wing into inner and outer halls, and turning some of the outbuildings into the banqueting hall where the Dufferins' tenants' ball was held, and the private chapel where their children were christened. It was a curious arrangement, the result of what Harold Nicolson called 'Lord Dufferin's optimism regarding his own capacity as an architect'.[6] Basil made few changes, apart from turning another outbuilding into a court for stické, an amalgam of squash and tennis which was a fashionable country house pastime in the early twentieth century. The house remained much as it was in the 1st Marquess's day, filled to the brim with souvenirs of his diplomatic career in Canada, Russia, Turkey and India where, as viceroy, he was responsible for the annexation of Burma in 1886. There were life-sized Indian and Burmese carvings 'which cause you to start wondering whether you had too much brandy for dinner,' declared one society gossip.[7] A stuffed Russian bear reared up out of the gloom in the outer hall, where he (or she) kept company with Egyptian deities carved in granite, Canadian curling stones, a mummy case, a rich assortment of knives, daggers, swords and pistols, and the stuffed head of a rhinoceros.

Pride of place in the inner hall was given to an enormous window filled with stained-glass heraldry. But in this room too there were relics of the 1st Marquess's career, including a stuffed walrus from Spitzbergen and an eight-foot-high totem that had once belonged to the Kwakiutl tribe of British Columbia. It had a scarlet head, blue horns and white fangs. According to Harold Nicolson, it also had draped around its waist, to shield delicate sensibilities from its rather prominent role as a fertility god, 'a loin-cloth of Malayan embroidery in which had once been wrapped a silver address box presented by the municipality of Rangoon'.[8] The overspill from Lord Dufferin's collections was housed in a new museum room. The remainder of the house, including the dining room, drawing room and a comfortable library, was more restful, although gods and weaponry still haunted corridors and reception rooms in a manner guaranteed to disconcert new guests.

Below
Just a few of Clandeboye's collection of remarkable relics acquired by the 1st Marquess.

Throughout the 1930s the society papers were full of the Dufferins' life at Clandeboye, picturing them with their children, their horses and their dogs 'at home in County Down'.[9] Maureen featured in *Country Life*, looking beautiful and beguiling in black and flanked by Caroline and Perdita, while she held up Sheridan for the world to admire. She appeared regularly in the *Tatler*, accompanied by guests at one of her 'outstandingly successful' house-parties.[10] In 1938 she was featured at the centre of a frankly peculiar photo-montage which surrounded her with what the caption described as 'her belongings'.[11] They included Clandeboye House; daughters Caroline and Perdita; a record player; Helen's Tower; her pet Pekingese, Puffin, and her horse, Corrida, 'who goes hunting with the County Down Staghounds'; and a toad. Apparently, she kept it as a pet.

Left
A 1938 *Tatler* photo-montage of Maureen surrounded by her favourite things, including her record player and her pet toad.

As far as the public was concerned, the Dufferins were one of the most glamorous couples in Britain. Maureen was seen at all the right parties, and was one of London's leading society hostesses. She was also well known for her practical jokes. House guests at Clandeboye would be bewildered to find her introducing them as someone else entirely, or offering them a wine glass with a hole in it, or fake plastic cheese. The story is often told of how she used to pretend to be a slovenly housemaid to welcome dinner guests at Hans Place. Less frequently reported is how, according to her granddaughter Ivana, she would arrive at social events wearing a false penis on her nose and a whoopee cushion hidden between her legs. How the other guests must have laughed.

Basil was busy carving out a political career for himself, first as Parliamentary Private Secretary to Lord Halifax and then, in 1937, as Under-Secretary of State for the Colonies. If he and Maureen led quite separate lives, that was not unusual for a wealthy young couple in the 1930s. At any one time, Basil might be shooting grouse in Scotland while Maureen was enjoying the delights of Biarritz; and their children remembered them both as very distant figures, who like the rest of their class left the child-rearing to others. But in fact, their marriage was failing. There were rumours that Maureen wanted a divorce so that she could marry the Duke of Devonshire who, as Marquess of Hartington, had stood as one of Caroline's godparents. Basil was drinking heavily and running up substantial debts, and telling people that *he* wanted a divorce from Maureen so that he could marry an American journalist, Virginia Cowle; but he couldn't pursue the matter because it would be the end of his political career.

Then came the war. Maureen did her bit, hosting fundraising dances and bridge parties at Clandeboye. The ten-year-old Lady Caroline Blackwood 'sold Victory matches', ran one report of a 350-strong party in aid of a local 'Victory Fund' which aimed to raise enough money to buy a Spitfire. 'Her sister, Lady Perdita, by means of a collecting box, raised a substantial sum.' Their three-and-a-half-year-old brother wandered around the tables looking cute in a tunic emblazoned with a huge 'V'.[12]

Basil joined the Guards in 1940. After being released to work in the Ministry of Information he rejoined and served in the Far East where on 25 March 1945, while he was working with the Indian Field Broadcasting Unit, he was killed by a Japanese mortar shell. Henry 'Chips' Channon, husband of Honor Guinness and thus the son-in-law of the Iveaghs, had taken Maureen's side in the Dufferins' pre-war marital problems, and he delivered a characteristically uncharitable valediction:

> I am sorry, as is everyone; but we all realise that it is a mercy. He was drunken, diseased, hopeless and feckless; his ambitions, his brain had been rotted by drink and corroded by money. Everybody praised and flattered him, for he was intelligent in many ways, but had no common sense, no design for living; and I was always concerned that he was rotten; he never did anything to dispel my view. For years now he has been a drunkard, unpunctual, ill, despicable and so revolting to look at that he took one's appetite away.[13]

His body was never recovered, and Maureen, with help from John Betjeman, put up a memorial stone, with lettering by Ninian Comper, in the family cemetery at Clandeboye. The inscription read, 'A man of brilliance and of many friends.' Betjeman composed a tender elegy to the friend of his youth, 'my kind heavy-lidded companion'.[14]

In 1948 Maureen married an ex-commando thirteen years her junior, Major Desmond 'Kelpie' Buchanan. They divorced six years later, and in 1955 she took as her third husband John Maude, a judge. The Maudes led separate lives, and Maureen kept her Dufferin and Ava title throughout these marriages and right up to her death in 1998. She also kept

Left
The staircase hall, known since the 1st Marquess's time as 'the gallery.'

Clandeboye, at least until 1968, when she handed it over to Sheridan and his wife Lindy, a Guinness cousin. And there is no question that she saved it, at a time when the British country house was going through the worst crisis in its history, with estate taxes running at 80 percent and sales and demolitions happening almost weekly. There was a moment when the future of Clandeboye hung in the balance, too. After Basil's death, it emerged that the estate had been heavily mortgaged to a Belfast solicitor to provide security for his gambling debts. There was also a dispute with trustees as to whether, when Basil left the demesne of Clandeboye to his widow until their son turned twenty-one, he meant the entire Dufferin estate, which included property all over County Down, or simply Clandeboye House. Trustees maintained the latter, and their view was upheld by the courts.

In effect, this would have left Maureen personally responsible for maintaining the house and grounds without any income from rents and profits. She responded by threatening that unless the courts would allow her to buy the mansion and all the lands within the demesne from the trustees, she would simply abandon Clandeboye and decamp to England, where she would buy herself another country house. They relented and she bought Clandeboye, for £192,000.

The death of her father Ernest Guinness in 1949 left Maureen very rich indeed, and she also received an income from the brewery, being one of the first Guinness women to be appointed to the board. (The other two were Honor and Patricia, daughters of Rupert, 2nd Earl of Iveagh.) Over the next ten years or so, she turned Clandeboye from a rather gloomy museum of a place into an elegant country house. In this, and like Aileen at Luttrellstown, she relied heavily on the services of Felix Harbord, whose talents as a designer she had experienced at her sister's various houses and parties.

By the early 1950s Harbord had become Maureen's party decorator of choice, too: when she hosted a ball at the Hurlingham Club in 1952 to celebrate Caroline's twenty-first birthday and to *début* Perdita, Harbord's decorations stole the show. Mermaids made of white flowers and holding sheafs of mauve gladioli hovered over mirrored walls, tapestries adorned the supper rooms, and hundreds of red candles in chandeliers provided the lighting. 'One guest, who goes to many of the big parties in Europe,' declared a breathless 'Jennifer' in the *Tatler*, 'told me that Mr Harbord's décor at Hurlingham for this ball was more beautiful and original than any he had seen.'[15] When Maureen gave a dinner-dance for Princess

Left
Perdita Blackwood, Caroline Blackwood and their mother Maureen, Marchioness of Dufferin and Ava, February 1955.

Margaret at Hans Place in 1953, people remarked on Harbord's settings (more mermaids, and a chandelier made of fresh flowers). When she organised a ball at the Hurlingham for Sheridan's coming-of-age in 1959, it was Harbord who draped the ballroom with a canopy of pale blue silk festooned with ivy and installed a night club, complete with illuminated walls, tiered seats and coloured lanterns around a tiny dance floor. The club and the rest of the paraphernalia were shipped over to Clandeboye for a repeat performance with a thousand guests a few weeks later.

As with Luttrellstown, it isn't always clear exactly what Felix Harbord did at Clandeboye, or even when, beyond the fact that he was working there off and on throughout the 1950s. The timeline is complicated still further by the fact that Sheridan and Lindy, the 5th Marquess and his marchioness, introduced decorative schemes of their own after Maureen handed over the house to them in 1968. We know that Harbord was at Clandeboye in April 1954, because that was when he noticed a dirty canvas partially obscuring the skylight in the 1st Marquess's museum room. He had it taken down and discovered that it was a picture of Jupiter and the nymph Calisto by François Boucher: it was later valued at £10,000, much to Maureen's delight.

It must have been around this time that Harbord was working up schemes for the three principal rooms on the east front: the saloon, the drawing room and the dining room. A screen of cream Ionic columns in the dining room was painted to resemble scagliola; the walls of the drawing room were painted a cerulean blue, and the room was given curtains of yellow silk; finicky mouldings were removed from niches in the saloon. Harbord also dealt in antiques, and he bought in items to suit the new interior schemes: a late eighteenth-century chimneypiece in the dining room; a gilt mirror over the fireplace in the drawing room. One of his last interventions was to design a Doric porte-cochère to relieve the rather forbiddingly plain entrance to the house. It was put up by Maureen to mark Sheridan's coming of age in 1959.

Right
The dining room, one of three rooms redecorated by Felix Harbord in the 1950s.

11

KELVEDON HALL

Essex

It was in April 1937, at a lunch party given by Sybil Colefax, that Henry 'Chips' Channon first heard that Kelvedon Hall, an early Georgian country house in Essex, was up for sale. 'I am intrigued, and shall look at and consider it,' he wrote in his diary. 'Will it prove only one more dream to toy with?' A few days later, on the spur of the moment he motored out of London to take a look at the house.

Opposite
John Spencer-Churchill's magical murals in the bathroom at Kelvedon, recently restored by Ashe Ericksson.

Below
The wedding of Honor Guinness and the socially ambitious Henry 'Chips' Channon, 1933.

Chicago-born Channon had married Lady Honor Guinness, daughter of the 2nd Earl of Iveagh, on 14 July 1933, three days after taking British citizenship. He was thirty-six, she was twelve years his junior. The marriage brought the socially ambitious Channon a seat in the House of Commons – his mother-in-law, who represented the Conservatives in the safe seat of Southend with a whopping majority, stood down in his favour in 1935. It also brought him another seat, this one as a director on the board of Guinness & Co.; his father-in-law made him a gift of £15,000-worth of Guinness shares, which enabled him to be elected to the board. And through Honor, it brought him access to the Guinness fortune. She had indulgent parents, and considerable wealth of her own.

In 1935, with help from Honor's parents, the Channons bought a London house, 5 Belgrave Square. It was a smart address – the Duke of Kent was a neighbour – and the Channons refurbished it in style. The *pièce de résistance*, a new dining room, was the work of Stéphane Boudin, then head of Maison

Above
Stéphane Boudin's dining room at the Channons' town house, 5 Belgrave Square.

Jansen in Paris and one of the most gifted of all the decorators at work around the mid-century. He is best known today for his work at the White House in the early 1960s for Jackie Kennedy. The interior he created for the Channons was loosely based on the Mirror Room in the Amalienburg, built for the Elector Karl Albert in the 1730s. It dripped with extravagantly opulent Rococo decoration, while the furniture included a silvered side table, silvered dining chairs and a mirror-topped dining table. 'A remarkable experience,' was the verdict of *Country Life*'s Christopher Hussey.[1] 'Very fine indeed,' Harold Nicolson told his wife, Vita Sackville-West: 'baroque and rococo and what-ho and oh-no-no and all that.'[2] 'It will shock, perhaps stagger London,' predicted a gleeful Channon. And 'it will cost us over £6,000.' In fact he reckoned that the whole Belgrave Square project would cost a colossal £40,000, although that didn't matter 'since the money seems to be there'.[3] 'There' being the Guinness family coffers.

The Kelvedon Hall estate had belonged to a Roman Catholic family, the Wrights, for 400 years, and it was John Wright who commissioned an unidentified architect to build him a new house around 1742. Another John Wright (there were ten generations of Johns) introduced some gentle neoclassical details about forty years later, but since then Kelvedon had escaped the attentions of modernisers. From the early 1920s, when it passed out of the Wright family, it had had a chequered history as a convent school and, apparently, a psychiatric institution. Two pupils had died from minor ailments, a woman had thrown herself from an upper window, and one of the sisters had drowned herself in the lake. Her ghost was said to float disconsolately around the gardens.

In early May 1937, Chips took Honor down to see Kelvedon with their architect, Gerald Wellesley. Chips had known Wellesley, whose father was the 4th Duke of Wellington, since the 1920s, and the firm of Wellesley and Trenwith Wills had filled 5 Belgrave Square with beautifully delicate neo-Regency interiors which were unfairly overshadowed by Boudin's wonderful but undeniably theatrical mirrored dining room. Gerry Wellesley was the obvious choice to advise the Channons on the options for Kelvedon, and his firm was the obvious choice to rescue it from its institutional past, if they decided to go ahead with the purchase.

It was a hot day, and the three of them explored the house and grounds, picnicked in the sun and talked over ideas. They found Kelvedon Hall remarkably untouched by both the twentieth and the nineteenth centuries: as one commentator put it a few years later, Honor and Chips 'had the rare pleasure of discovering an almost unrecorded Georgian mansion of a high order of merit in practically untouched condition'.[4] It was a plain, almost austere building – on the outside, at least. Built of warm red brick, it consisted of a central block, seven bays wide and three storeys high, with flanking pavilions which stood forward of the main block and which were connected to it by quadrant screen walls. The interiors were a beautiful mixture of English Rococo and a restrained, Adamesque neoclassicism.

'The place has infinite charm,' said Chips after a second visit, again with Gerry Wellesley; 'but [it] wants a great deal done to it.'[5] There was also the phantom nun to consider; and the Channons were uneasy enough about her to ask the Right Reverend Arthur Doubleday, Roman Catholic Bishop of Brentwood, for his help in laying the ghost. But they decided to buy Kelvedon, or rather Chips did. Honor's contribution was indirect and largely financial. The couple motored down to Pyrford Court one Sunday in May and told the Iveaghs they wanted the house, and Lord Iveagh simply told them that the family solicitors would arrange things. The next day Chips contacted the lawyers and discovered that two months earlier Lord Iveagh had set up a trust of £52,000 for his daughter – just in case she ever wanted a country house. There and then, Chips contacted the agents and made an offer of £5,000 for the Hall.

Gerry Wellesley was put in charge of the refurbishment, with help from the society decorator Dolly Mann, who had worked for Honor's cousin Bryan Guinness at Biddesden. (Sybil Colefax, at whose luncheon party Chips had first heard about Kelvedon, was put out not to get the job.) Window frames and sills were painted a striking turquoise blue. The drawing room was given grey walls, pink and grey upholstery and an Aubusson carpet. The dining room was sage-green. A garden room with butter-yellow walls had a white and green marble chimneypiece, the only one that wasn't original to the house. In pride of place over it was a hunting scene by John Wootton, a present to Chips from Honor

Below
A plaster dove hovers over Honor's bed in the converted chapel.

Above
The landing: Honor was happy to let her husband take the lead in matters of taste.

to mark their fifth wedding anniversary. The Wrights' domestic oratory was converted into Honor's bedroom, its walls painted duck-egg blue and her ornate crimson damask bed (with curtains to match) placed in an alcove where the altar once was, while a plasterwork dove of the Holy Spirit hovered above it, presiding over her sleeping.

Kelvedon's delightfully neo-Georgian character was interrupted here and there. In the grounds, the Channons installed a swimming pool with a bizarre Baroque bathing pavilion, designed by Austrian art director William Kellner. More successfully, the walls and ceiling of Honor's octagonal bathroom, which led off her chapel bedroom, were festooned with huge painted monkeys swinging from palm trees, endlessly reflected in a series of artfully positioned mirrors.

The artist responsible for this mural was John Spencer-Churchill, the nephew of Winston. Seven years before, Channon had been responsible for Johnny opting to leave his staid and boring job with a Stock Exchange firm to embark on the uncertain life of a mural artist. Having executed a vast and sprawling set of architectural and landscape scenes

Above
William Kellner's Baroque bathing pavilion.

Opposite
The swimming pool, with Kelvedon's formal gardens beyond.

which covered his tolerant mother's drawing room and flowed out and up the stairs, and receiving some general encouragement from some of his parents' guests, including Sir Edwin Lutyens and Sir John Lavery, in 1931 he was offered a hundred pounds by Channon to paint a fresco round the latter's dining room at his flat in Gloucester Place. 'I want it to depict my friends arriving at a fabulous party,' Chips told him. 'Make it an Italian setting.'

That was enough to convince Churchill to leave his job. His first commission had a short life – when Chips married Honor he sold the lease on the Gloucester Place flat, and the new occupant told Johnny the mural was so frightful that he had it destroyed. But Johnny gradually established his reputation, with help from his family: he decorated the loggia in the garden at Uncle Winston's Chartwell, for example, with scenes from the campaigns of their mutual ancestor, John Churchill,

Duke of Marlborough. And Channon remembered that Gloucester Place mural. In May 1938 he took Johnny down to Kelvedon, where he spent the summer painting Honor's coconut grove bathroom. He also executed a curious little fresco over the door of the Kelvedon orangery, depicting the twelve signs of the zodiac. He was, said Chips, a 'dear gentle creature, far cleverer really than any of the Churchills'.[6]

By now there were more than a hundred men at work on Kelvedon, the house and grounds. Channon, who had a very high opinion of his own abilities when it came to matters of artistic taste, continued to take the lead in making decisions over the interiors, while Honor left him to it. He complained that she took no interest in Kelvedon, although in reality he wouldn't have welcomed any interference with his grand plans for the house. As these neared completion, with colour-schemes decided and painters already at work executing them, there was trouble over one of the few pieces of entirely new architecture – a pair of entrance lodges designed by Wellesley and his partner, Trenwith Wills. Low, balustraded, with niches for classical urns, they stood to either side of the drive and

Below
The drawing room. A portrait by Herbert James Gunn of Chips with the Channons' son Paul hangs over the fireplace.

were linked by a taller triumphal arch. The whole composition was rendered in white stucco and had an elegantly Regency air.

Unfortunately, Essex County Council decided the lodges were ugly, and for a while refused planning permission. It took a furious Wellesley several months to show the Council the error of its ways, and in the meantime Honor and Chips were both feeling increasingly exasperated at the lack of progress on the restoration of the house itself. Wellesley 'has neglected Kelvedon in the most scandalous and expensive manner,' said Chips, ranting that his old friend was pompous and unhelpful.[7] By the middle of June the friend had become 'that fiend', and was being blamed for the fact that the couple still couldn't move in.[8]

The Channons took up residence at Kelvedon that summer; although their interests still lay in London, and the Belgrave Square house remained their home. But relations with their architect deteriorated to such an extent that they broke with Gerry Wellesley in 1939 and would have nothing more to do with him. He gave up his architectural practice four years later when he inherited a dukedom and a ducal palace, Stratfield Saye, as 7th Duke of Wellington.

Kelvedon Hall was not destined to be a happy house for either of the Channons. Chips never quite knew what to make of Honor, who didn't share his vast social ambitions and was, one suspects, rather bored with his pretentions. The daughter of an earl didn't need to engage in the kind of lion-hunting at which her husband excelled. The daughter of a Guinness had even less need of it. Chips was more at home with her parents, who both doted on him. Honor is more of a mystery than Chips, who wore his pretensions and prejudices on his sleeve. She was quite a bluestocking in her younger days; and after her marriage the society papers were fulsome in their praise of her talents as a hostess, while quick to note her disdain for convention. She caused a sensation in the summer of 1934 at a big Guinness dinner party when the guest of honour was the Duchess of York (later Queen Elizabeth, and later still the Queen Mother). Honor, said the press, was 'very beautifully gowned and bejewelled – even to a massive tiara – but with no stockings.'[9] Still, as one gossip columnist put it, 'Lady Honor can afford to do anything her fancy takes.'[10]

After the birth of the Channons' only child, Paul, in October 1935, Honor's fancy took her out of their marriage. She grew increasingly moody and bored with her husband, and one reason for her lack of interest in Kelvedon was an affair with a handsome ski instructor named Bron. When he was killed in a mountaineering accident in the Alps in

Overleaf
Kelvedon Hall.

the summer of 1938, she broke down, got drunk and confessed the affair to her husband. She also had a brief affair with a four-times married Hungarian adventurer, Count 'Pali' von Erdödi-Pálffy. 'I don't think she loves me now,' wrote Chips, poignantly.[11]

In 1940 he began to notice that she was spending a lot of time with the Kelvedon land agent, a married man called Frank Woodman. 'She allows herself to be so familiar with that sort of people,' he complained.[12] But he said nothing, hoping the liaison would blow itself out. However, by this time the bisexual Chips had almost certainly embarked on an

Below
The library.

affair himself – with Peter Coats, a young Scot who would become his companion and partner for the rest of his life, and whom his enemies nicknamed 'Petticoats'. Honor loathed Coats. 'She must have some feminine intuition about him,' said Chips.[13] Whether she did or not, the presence of Coats didn't do much to help their failing marriage.

In October 1940, Honor told her husband that she wanted a divorce so that she could marry Woodman. Mortified, perhaps because he still had feelings for her, but also because she was committing social suicide by running off with someone 'of the yeoman class', and ruining his chances of a peerage – 'like Lady Chatterley in every respect,' said a gleeful Evelyn Waugh when he heard the news – Chips went for help to his in-laws, who responded by hiring detectives to inquire into Woodman's character.[14] Their report was not encouraging, but Honor was determined to leave her husband, her Belgrave Square house and Kelvedon Hall. She bought a farm near Winchester where she lived 'in squalor and sin,' said a bitter Chips, until she and Woodman tired of each other.[15] In 1946 she married a Czech RAF pilot, Frank Svejdar, remaining with him until her death thirty years later. In another break with family tradition, she converted to Catholicism, the first of the Guinnesses to do so.

Chips kept up his good relationship with the Iveaghs. He also kept Belgrave Square and Kelvedon Hall. In March 1941, on his forty-fourth birthday, he entertained Christopher Hussey at Kelvedon. Hussey was preparing a laudatory article on the house for *Country Life*, and Channon enjoyed showing off what he regarded as his own creation. But when Hussey left, he broke down. Kelvedon was Heartbreak House, he declared. There were piles of unopened letters; the gardens were neglected; the servants didn't know what was happening and Honor's dogs were uncared for. 'I can't bear to live any more,' he wrote in his diary. 'There is only void, separation, loneliness and disappointment ahead of me.'[16]

12

LUGGALA

County Wicklow

The Lovin' Spoonful were on stage in the marquee, doing their best to play 'Daydream', their latest hit. Unfortunately, the band was so stoned that they were having trouble with their instruments, and the performance was rocky rather than rocking. Meanwhile, Brian Jones had been dropping acid for most of the weekend. He sat cross-legged on the floor, watching the band and clutching his sitar, while his girlfriend Anita Pallenberg, who was also tripping, gazed at him adoringly. Mick Jagger was having a row with *his* girlfriend, Chrissie Shrimpton, over the lyrics to the Stones' latest album, *Aftermath*. She was convinced that dismissive lines in 'Out of Time' referred to her. Elsewhere, designer David Mlinaric talked to David Dimbleby; Paul McCartney's brother Mike was discussing Magritte with art collector Sir Alfred Beit. In a corner of the drawing room, a Nigerian conga player called Jimmy Scott played the bongos.

Opposite
Luggala's setting by Lough Tay is glorious.

Below
Philip de Laszlo's beguiling portrait of Golden Guinness Girl Oonagh, 1931.

Oonagh, Lady Oranmore and Browne was throwing a party.

Oonagh was the youngest of Ernest Guinness's three Golden Girls. And the party, held in April 1966 to mark the coming of age of her youngest son Tara, was taking place at one of the Guinness family's most magical country houses: Luggala, an outrageously pretty Gothick castle in a remote and

stunningly beautiful setting on the shore of Lough Tay, high up in the Wicklow Hills.

Luggala began life at the end of the eighteenth century as a simple shooting box belonging to a Dublin banking family named La Touche. The La Touches' main residence was Bellevue House, ten miles away, and Luggala was a retreat where Peter La Touche, who bought the estate in 1788, could indulge his passion for shooting and fishing. We don't know the name of Luggala's architect, or even exactly when La Touche decided to turn a rather ordinary little lodge into the exquisite battlemented toy that stands there today. Referred to simply as a 'modern built house' in 1796, it was not until 1822 that a visitor noted that it was built 'with excellent taste, and in the pointed style'.[1]

By the early twentieth century, the La Touches had sold the 5000-acre Luggala estate, which now belonged to the 8th Viscount Powerscourt. Facing mounting expenses without the funds to meet them, Lord Powerscourt happily let the lodge to Ernest Guinness, and his three girls spent happy summers there, swimming in the lough and

Below
Luggala: built 'with excellent taste, and in the pointed style'.

Above
Oonagh models a ready-to-wear tweed suit and straw hat for Fortnum & Mason, 1933.

entertaining their friends. Daphne Vivian, leading light of the Bright Young Things and soon to be the wife of Viscount Thynne, heir to the Longleat estates, recalled a visit in 1925. 'Most of the day we spent by the lake in dressing-gowns and pyjamas, fancying that we looked like the photographs we had seen in *The Tatler* of smart people at the Lido.'[2] It was at Luggala that Viscount Thynne proposed to her.

In June 1929 Oonagh, who was described at her coming-out as the loveliest girl in London, was married in a blaze of publicity at St Margaret's Westminster. She was just nineteen and her husband Philip, youngest son of the 1st Baron Kindersley, was twenty. For a time, they seemed to be the perfect couple. Full-page photographs of Oonagh appeared in the *Bystander* and the *Tatler*, where 'one of the most charming of Society's Younger Brigade' was accompanied by her two French bulldogs sporting mink collars.[3] The Kindersleys had a son, Gay, a year after the wedding, and a daughter, Tessa, in 1932. But the marriage was not a success. Philip didn't like Ireland: his father-in-law's Glenmaroon was not to his taste, and he thought Luggala was a god-forsaken place in the middle of nowhere. But he did like one of Oonagh's bridesmaids – rather too much, as it turned out. The affair with Valerie, Lady Brougham and Vaux, was soon the talk of London society, and Oonagh sought consolation in the arms of an Anglo-Irish aristocrat, Dominick Browne, 4th Lord Oranmore and Browne.* Browne was married with five children, and after a messy series of divorces, in which Philip Kindersley rather unsportingly sued Oonagh for divorce on the grounds of his wife's adultery with Dominick,

* The Oranmore and Browne peerage was Irish, but Browne also had an English title, Baron Mereworth, which enabled him to sit in the House of Lords – and he did, for seventy-two years. 'He earned the unspoken admiration of many by never speaking in the chamber,' according to his obituary (*Daily Telegraph*, 10 August 2002, p. 23.)

Left
Oonagh with her second husband, Dominick, 4th Lord Oranmore and Browne.

and Dominick's wife sued him for adultery citing Oonagh, the pair were married in 1936.

To mark the marriage, Ernest Guinness bought the leased Luggala estate from Lord Powerscourt and presented it to his youngest daughter as a wedding present. 'Luggala has been given to me by my kind father to share with Dom, Gay and Tessa,' she wrote in her visitors' book in June 1937.[4] Dominick tried to join up when war broke out, but he was advised that he would better aid the war effort if he stuck to farming his estate, and the couple remained in Ireland, dividing their time between Luggala, Glenmaroon, and Castle MacGarrett, the Browne family's ancestral seat in County Mayo. Oonagh had three more children: Garech, born in 1939; an unnamed baby who died within days; and Tara, her last child, who was born in 1945.

The late 1940s were a difficult time for Oonagh. Her daughter by Philip Kindersley, Tessa, died suddenly in 1946 after suffering an anaphylactic reaction to a vaccination for diptheria. She was buried by the lake at Luggala, next to 'Baby Browne'. Three years later Ernest Guinness died, leaving his daughters not quite as well off as they had hoped: although he had made over a substantial part of his fortune to them in an effort to avoid heavy death duties, he died too soon, with those gifts still liable for tax.

To cap it all, Oonagh's second marriage was failing, and Dominick had fallen in love with a movie starlet named Sally Gray. There is a story that while Oonagh and Dominick were staying at Luggala one weekend, she suggested they sail on Lough Tay alone, away from guests and children. Out on the lake, she told him that if he didn't end the affair immediately, their marriage was over. He didn't, and Oonagh was granted a decree nisi in July 1950. She retired to Luggala, which would become her main residence for the next 20 years.

Below
Brendan Behan enjoying Luggala's famous hospitality.

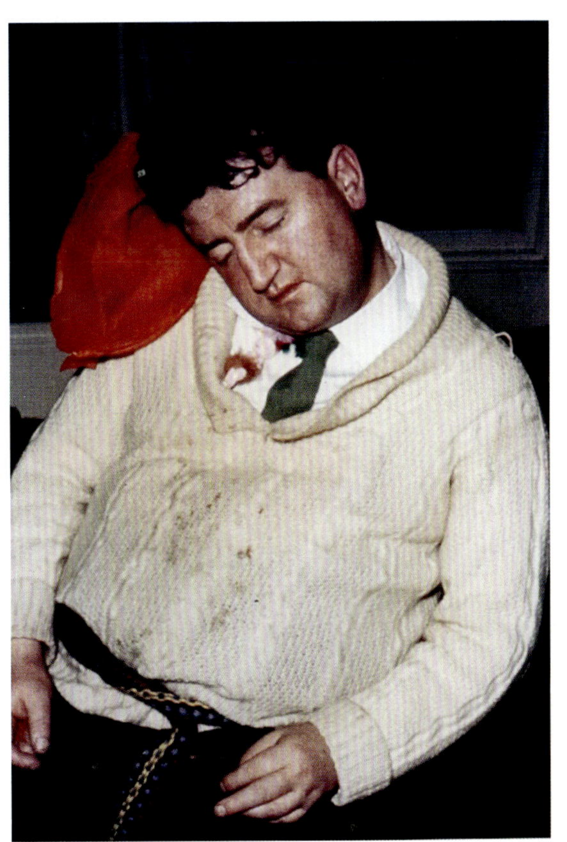

But if this all suggests that Lady Oranmore and Browne was some kind of tragic heroine, left in the remoteness of Luggala to mourn her fate like a latter-day Lady of Shalott, nothing could be further from the truth. Independent for the first time in her life, she began to entertain – who she wanted, how she wanted and when she wanted. 'Oonagh somehow imbued Luggala with enchantment,' recalled her friend, the writer Michael Luke.[5] Nobody could keep away, he went on – artists and poets and film stars and intellectuals were all drawn to the little piece of Strawberry Hill Gothick in the Wicklow Hills. 'And the still centre of this exultant, exuberant chaos was Oonagh.'

Brendan Behan was one regular houseguest, having been introduced to Oonagh by another friend, Lucian Freud. Behan was a fixture at her Christmas house parties, and Oonagh would send her Rolls-Royce down into Dublin to collect him and, after his marriage in 1955, his wife Beatrice. Photographs from the time show him, bleary-eyed and tie askew, proposing a toast at the dinner table, or chatting with Oonagh and Beatrice, or dead drunk and fast asleep in a chair while the party carried on around him. Screenwriter Peter Viertel remembered taking the actor Michael Wilding to dinner at Luggala one Christmas Eve. (Wilding's wife Elizabeth Taylor should have been there too, but she had just deserted her husband for Victor Mature.) At the end of the meal Behan staggered to his feet, proposed a toast 'to her ladyship, God bless her!' and fell forward onto the dinner table, which collapsed. 'Oh dear,' was all Oonagh said. 'Time for us to move back into the drawing room.'[6] Later that night Behan woke up, sang 'O Come, All Ye Faithful' and fell down the backstairs.

The film director John Huston was another frequent visitor and a good friend to Oonagh, although on his first visit to the house in 1951, he discovered that invitations to Luggala weren't always what they seemed. The only book on his bedside table that first night was Claud Cockburn's *Beat the Devil*, a thriller written under the pseudonym James Helvick. The next day Huston found that other copies of this book had been left at strategic points around the house. Whether that was Cockburn's doing, or Oonagh's, the stratagem worked: Huston read the book and liked it. He persuaded Humphrey Bogart to buy the rights, and directed Bogart and Jennifer Jones in the film adaptation, with a script from Truman Capote.

By the early 1950s Oonagh had embarked on a long affair with the journalist and historian Robert Kee, and perhaps it was through Kee that his old friends, the Bloomsburyites Francis and Ralph Partridge, stayed a night at Luggala in August 1952. They had not visited before, and they immediately found themselves enjoying the tail-end of a week-long house party, in company with Kee and Oonagh; Daphne Vivian, now Daphne Thynne, but soon to leave her name and her husband, the Marquess of Bath; Claud Cockburn and his wife Patricia; and Lucian Freud and his wife Kitty, daughter of Jacob Epstein. Freud would shortly leave Kitty and elope to Paris with the writer Caroline Blackwood, Oonagh's niece, who preferred her aunt's company to that of her mother and who was another regular guest both before and after her elopement. In her diary Frances Partridge captured perfectly the warm, welcoming, slightly fey atmosphere of the place, the way in which one immediately felt at ease:

> The front door was opened and we were at once in the hall-dining-room, where a huge fire blazed and an oval table laid for dinner filled nearly all the space. What a magical atmosphere that house had, charmingly furnished and decorated to match its style, dim lights,

soft music playing and Irish voices ministering seductively to our needs. In the drawing-room stood Oonagh with her hair down her back, and in her short diaphanous dress looking exactly like the fairy off a Christmas tree.[7]

Luggala's remote location, 26 miles from Dublin, meant that Oonagh had problems keeping staff. The situations vacant columns of Irish newspapers of the 1960s are peppered with advertisements for cooks, maids, and chauffeurs. 'Man capable of handling Rolls Royce an advantage,' ran one.[8] The one constant presence in her household was her butler, Patrick Cummins, who shimmers effortlessly through a dozen memoirs,

Below
A disastrous fire all but destroyed Luggala in January 1956.

organising transport, waiting at table, putting drunks to bed and generally easing his mistress's way through life. When she broke up with Dominick Oranmore and Browne, she is said to have exclaimed, 'Never mind. Cummins didn't ever like him much.'[9]

Cummins was seen at his awesome best in the aftermath of a disastrous fire that broke out at Luggala one night in January 1956, destroying most of the house. Robert Kee, who was staying with Oonagh, stood on the lawn, hypnotised by the flickering flames – until he remembered that all his belongings and money were still in the house, a fact which spurred him on to help with the firefighting. But it was Cummins who organised the evacuation, getting his mistress, Garech and Tara and Gay Kindersley and his fiancée Margaret Wakefield to safety before fighting his way through blinding smoke and flames to telephone for help before the line went. Then, ignoring the explosions from dozens of bottles of champagne in the cellar (Veuve Clicquot 1947, according to one of Oonagh's friends), he went back into the burning house to rescue photograph albums, family pictures and other irreplaceable items.

Oonagh immediately decided to rebuild, using the Dublin architect Alan Hope and the London decorators Green and Abbott. But it took time. The Irish peer John Kilbracken took an American friend to see the ruined house several months after the fire. As they pulled up, they saw the full extent of the disaster. The roof had gone, and they could glimpse blue sky through the blackened windows. Rubble and debris littered the interiors 'in a maze of dereliction'.[10]

Suddenly Patrick Cummins appeared, immaculate in his white jacket and perfectly creased trousers. 'Good evening, m'lord. Did you wish to see her ladyship?' It turned out that Oonagh, who was living in Paris while the damage was assessed and repaired, had come home for the day and was taking tea with Tara in one of the cowsheds. 'Would you care to join them?'[11]

In June 1960 a notice appeared in the Irish press:

> Mrs Ferreras, Luggala, Roundwood, Co. Wicklow will open her garden and house in aid of the Jubilee Nurses' Pension Fund on Sunday next (3 to 6 pm). Admission to grounds, 1/6; to house 2/6, tea. An old Irish kitchen full of antiques will be on view.[12]

Quite what the old Irish kitchen full of antiques was doing there is anyone's guess. But Mrs Ferreras was Oonagh, who had jettisoned her Oranmore and Browne title in 1957 and married Miguel Ferreras, a Spanish-Cuban-American with an uncertain past which varied from time to time, and which may or may not have involved fighting with the Waffen-SS on the Eastern Front. With the build of a boxer, he could certainly be quite physical on occasion: once during a Christmas house party at Luggala he suddenly accused the drunken Brendan Behan of molesting Oonagh's teenage son Tara, dragged him outside and beat him up. Oonagh, who didn't believe the accusation for a moment, came out, wrapped the bloodied and bruised Behan in a Foxford Mills blanket and led him gently back into the house.

Ferreras claimed to be a dress designer, although Nancy Mitford reported that he would have been better off opening a flower shop. Nevertheless, Oonagh invested heavily in a lavish white salon for her husband on the Rue de la Faubourg St Honoré, where he set himself up as a couturier and began exhibiting his designs during Paris fashion week. In the summer of 1964, the glamorous couple announced to the world that they were planning to adopt twin babies from Mexico.

Right
Tara Browne, Oonagh's youngest son.

A few weeks later Oonagh announced that she wanted a divorce. It isn't clear why: perhaps because she had discovered that he was using his dead brother's identity, perhaps because he was being unfaithful. Either way, the story made front page news. 'I don't know what has got into her,' an injured Ferreras told *France Dimanche*, although he seems to have been most upset by the fact that she wanted her money back and he would have to close his salon.[13] But he swiftly married another heiress, becoming the eighth husband of Flora Trujillo, the daughter of assassinated Dominican dictator Rafael Trujillo; while Oonagh ran the salon herself for a short time before giving it up. She kept the twins, and reverted to calling herself Lady Oranmore and Browne, a title she kept for the rest of her life.

Luggala was not her only home. At one time she owned a villa at Cap d'Antibes, 'La Jolie', where she kept up her practice of lavish hospitality. 'Sparkling, wildly generous and totally lovable' was the verdict of one of her neighbours, who also reckoned that her house guests seemed to include half the Irish cabinet and recalled that on one occasion when she invited Oonagh to lunch, the latter asked if she might bring 'a few friends' and turned up with fourteen.[14] She also had another villa in Bermuda, and an apartment on the shores of Lake Geneva. But until she made it over to her son Garech in 1970, Luggala was her main residence. In the summer of 1965, she hosted what the invitations called a 'pique nique', a charity lunch in the Luggala gardens. Around 300 guests sat under the trees or down by the lake, eating picnic lunches from baskets filled with chicken, cold meats, fruit, cheese and champagne, while the Chieftains played to entertain them.[15] 'Even by the standards of Irish gregariousness,' wrote the columnist Kenneth Rose, in Ireland in 1966 to interview Oonagh's eldest son Gay Kindersley, who was pursuing a career as a jump jockey, 'Luggala offers a warmth of welcome and ease of routine that are supremely memorable.'[16]

In April 1966 Tara Browne celebrated his twenty-first birthday with one of Luggala's last great parties. Tara was more comfortable in Chelsea or Carnaby Street than rural Ireland. A lover of fast cars, he had a turquoise Lotus Elan and an AC Cobra that was painted in psychedelic colours. He gave Paul McCartney his first experience with LSD. A dedicated follower of fashion, he was planning to go down that archetypal Swinging London route by opening a boutique on the King's Road. And he was already married with two small children, although by the time of the party he and his wife Nicky were not getting on. She blamed Oonagh, who disapproved of the match and, according to Nicky, did her best to break it up.

For the party, the Brownes leased two Caravelle passenger jets to bring guests over to Ireland from London and Paris. 'Beats go on pilgrimage to Guinness party,' ran one headline.[17] 'I just remember this mass of androgynous youth moving towards the terminal building,' said Christopher Gibbs, the Old Etonian antiques dealer and interior designer.[18] Nicky Browne was with Brian Jones and Anita Pallenberg: the three of them had taken acid on the plane, and they were already tripping as they were driven into the Wicklow hills.

The marquee in the grounds was decorated by David Mlinaric. There were coloured lights in the trees. Oonagh, who floated serenely through the crowds in a pink satin ballgown, was said to have flown The Lovin' Spoonful over from New York especially, at a cost of $10,000. In fact,

Right
The Lovin' Spoonful.

the band was already in England to promote their new album, and the cost – which Tara said he paid – was just under £1,000. He had first heard their 'Do You Believe in Magic?' when his friend Brian Jones brought him the record back from America. 'I thought it was fabulous,' said Tara. 'I like the group so much I couldn't miss the opportunity.'[19] When they arrived at Luggala, they were met by their host in a black velvet suit; he set them at their ease by offering each a lump of hash and a pipe. They may not have played so well on the night, but they certainly enjoyed themselves. Drummer Joe Butler recalled making love to a girl in a field, and riding horses, and seeing rainbows. 'If you asked me to sum up the Sixties in a single moment,' he said, 'then I would just describe the weekend of Tara Browne's twenty-first birthday party.'[20]

A week before Christmas 1966 Tara was driving a girlfriend in a borrowed Lotus Elan through London in the early hours of the morning,

Left
Tara's psychedelic AC Cobra.

Above
Oonagh's son Garech.

when he lost control and crashed into a parked van. The woman was unhurt, but he died from his injuries.

Brian Jones wept when he heard. Anita Pallenberg named a child she had with Keith Richard 'Tara'. John Lennon and Paul McCartney wrote the song 'A Day in the Life'. Oonagh buried her son at Luggala, next to Tessa. It was raining so hard that a hydraulic pump was brought in to prevent the grave from filling with water.

In 1970 Oonagh made over Luggala to her son Garech and went to live in the south of France.

13 CASTLETOWN HOUSE

County Kildare

Opposite
Castletown House.

In March 1965 an advertisement appeared in *Country Life*, announcing the sale by auction of Castletown House in County Kildare, 'without doubt the finest example of Georgian architecture in Ireland,' declared the agents.[1] And for once, that was no exaggeration. Castletown was, and is, a masterpiece, arguably the most important country house in Ireland.

It was built between 1722 and 1729 for William Conolly, whose meteoric rise to fame and fortune rivals that of a Guinness. Born in Donegal in 1662, the son of a Protestant inn-keeper who was prosperous enough to send the boy off to study law in Dublin, William began buying up forfeited estates in the aftermath of the Williamite Wars of 1689–91. He soon had properties in ten counties, and by 1715, when he was chosen Speaker in the Irish Parliament – a position he held until his death in 1729 – he was one of the richest, if not *the* richest, commoner in Ireland.

Below
The builder: William 'Speaker' Conolly (1662–1729).

And everything Speaker Conolly did was on a massive scale. His fortune was huge. His town house on Dublin's fashionable Capel Street was bigger than all the rest. And the sweeping façade of Castletown House, a thoroughly Palladian palazzo consisting of a central main block flanked by curving Ionic colonnades leading to matching pavilions, was 60 ft high and a jaw-dropping 400 ft long.

Opposite
The staircase hall.

There has always been some confusion about who was responsible for the design of Castletown. But it is generally agreed today that the monumental façade was by the Italian Alessandro Galilei, who met Conolly when he visited Ireland in 1718–19. Galilei was back in Italy when work on Conolly's mansion got under way, and the interiors may have been the work of young Edward Lovett Pearce, who would go on – with support from Speaker Conolly – to design the new Irish Parliament House on College Green in Dublin. But Castletown was nowhere near finished at Conolly's death: when the travel-writer John Loveday visited three years later, in 1732, he remarked that it was 'much the grandest house we have seen in Ireland', while noting that there wasn't much furniture, and work on the main staircase had not even started.[2] In fact the staircase hall, which predictably holds one of the largest staircases in Ireland, remained a shell until 1759, when it was completed by the Anglo-Dutch stone carver Simon Vierpyl, with Rococo plasterwork by the Swiss stuccadore Philip Lafranchini.

By the middle of the twentieth century the Castletown estate belonged to a Major Edward Conolly. On his death in 1956 it was inherited by his nephew, Patrick Conolly-Carew, 7th Baron Carew. And it was Carew who decided to sell up in 1965, admitting that although 'one just hates giving it up ... I just can't afford to keep the place alive.'[3]

The auction was held on 19 May 1965 in the main hall at Castletown. There were six bidders, some of them foreign: the Italian Ambassador was there, as was the Cultural Attaché at the German Embassy, who was representing a German business syndicate. After a tense round of bidding, the house and 580 acres went for £166,000 to a young Englishman, Julian De Lisle, and his cousin, Major James Wilson, the Master of the Kildare Hunt. De Lisle told reporters that he intended to live in part of the mansion, and that while nothing about its future was fixed, there were plans to hold horse trials on the estate. The following year, 1966, the house was the setting for a three-day sale of the contents, as Major Wilson announced that he and his wife were going to move in, and that Castletown was to be converted into a hotel. Parts of the estate were sold off to private developers. Neither the Wilsons nor De Lisle seem to have lived in the house, and quite soon it fell victim to vandals. Lead disappeared from the roof; windows were smashed. A sad fate for the grandest house in Ireland.

What has all this to do with the Guinness family? One thing, and one thing only: in April 1967 the Irish newspapers carried a report that Castletown House had been sold again, along with its remaining 110 acres. The price was £93,000, and the buyers were Desmond Guinness and his wife Mariga.

Born in 1931, Desmond Guinness was the second son of Bryan Guinness, Lord Moyne, and his first wife Diana Mitford.* He met Princess Hermione Marie-Gabrielle Petronella Sophia Devota Florestine of Urach, always known as Mariga, a contraction of Marie-Gabrielle, at Oxford in 1951. They were introduced by Prince Rupert Löwenstein, Mariga's cousin who was later to find fame of a sort as the Rolling Stones' business adviser; and in 1954 they were married in Christ Church Cathedral, Oxford.

A year or so later, the newly-weds moved to Carton House in County Kildare. Designed by Richard Castle in 1739, the vast ancestral seat of the Dukes of Leinster had been bought in 1949 by the wealthy Conservative politician and wartime Nazi sympathiser Arthur Nall-Cain, 2nd Lord Brocket, who, since he already owned country houses in Hertfordshire and Hampshire, as well as extensive estates in Scotland, was happy to let his latest acquisition. (Given Brocket's background, one can't help wondering, on no basis at all, whether Desmond having Oswald Mosley as a stepfather played a part in the arrangement.) The Guinnesses were on the lookout for a farm in good hunting territory – Desmond was an enthusiastic foxhunter – but during their stay there, which lasted until the end of 1957, they spent a lot of their time just exploring Ireland and nurturing their mutual concern for the future of the country's rich architectural heritage. One result of that voyage of discovery was that in July 1957 Desmond Guinness wrote to *The Irish Times*, noting that the old Georgian Society, founded in 1908, had fallen into abeyance, and asking if anyone would mind if he resurrected it. His aims, he said, were to update the Society's photographic records; to publish; and to 'fight for the preservation of what is left of Georgian architecture in Ireland'.[4]

The very idea of preserving historic buildings in Ireland was fraught with problems in the 1950s and 1960s. A lack of a proper protective listing system, the difficulties and immense costs involved in maintaining a big

* James Lees-Milne remembered being introduced to Desmond Guinness over lunch one day. 'I wish Bryan would not go on having more children,' he told Lees-Milne. 'The money won't go round at this rate.' He was thirteen at the time, and his father and stepmother had three children. They clearly paid no heed to Desmond, since they went on to produce six more. (Lees-Milne 1984, p. 201.)

country house and a demand by developers for space in cities and towns all played a part in the demolitions that were taking place all over the country. But there was something more insidious: a conviction that the past – especially the colonial past – had no place in modern Irish society. And there was an inescapable sense among certain sections of the population that a Castletown or a Dublin street filled with elegant Georgian houses was a relic of colonial oppression, something to be swept away rather than cherished, along with the landed class that had once enjoyed it. When two important early Georgian houses on Kildare Place in Dublin were demolished in 1957, a government minister notoriously declared that 'I was glad to see them go. They stood for everything I hate.'[5]

The new Irish Georgian Society, led by Desmond and Mariga Guinness, fought against that prejudice (although their fight wasn't helped by the fact that they and many of their comrades in the IGS came from the kind of backgrounds that were being criticised). In 1958, the Guinnesses put their money where their mouths were and bought their own historic house, Leixlip Castle, which stood four miles south-east of Carton, and a couple of miles from Castletown. The Conollys of Castletown had once owned it and used it occasionally when work was being carried out at the main house.

Leixlip was hardly an untouched example of pure Georgian: a Norman round tower loomed over a medieval core, and there were Regency battlements and some interesting Jacobethan work installed in the early twentieth century. But there was enough of the eighteenth century to intrigue and excite: mid-eighteenth-century additions, including a library and drawing room; some Rococo plasterwork; charming and romantic Gothick details. Just as exciting were the Guinnesses' ideas of decorating and furnishing the place, using bold colours, big Irish furniture, chimneypieces and doorcases that were salvaged from Georgian houses that were being demolished all over the country in the late 1950s and 1960s. Nancy Mitford, Desmond's aunt, declared Leixlip to be 'the epitome of civilised taste'.[6] John Cornforth claimed that it defined the post-war country house look just as Ditchley Park and Kelmarsh had defined it in the 1930s.

With Leixlip serving as the IGS's headquarters, Desmond, the Society's chair, campaigned and argued and wrote books and conducted endless lecture tours, particularly in America, which he rightly recognised as fertile ground when it came to seeking financial support for his cause. Following British examples, he emphasised the economic

value of historic buildings as employment opportunities and tourist attractions; in 1961 he launched the Irish Country House Owners' Representative Committee, which lobbied for tax breaks and government grants for maintenance. At the time, the Board of Works could only make grants for repairing historic homes if they had no roofs, which was a case if there ever was one of shutting the stable door after the horse had bolted.

Opposite
The famous long gallery.

Right
The Pompeian decoration, which dates from the 1770s, is the work of the English artist Charles Ruben Riley.

Left
Desmond Guinness plays host to Princess Margaret and Lord Snowdon, 1965.

Mariga was just as energetic in the cause. Christopher Gibbs remembered how she would lead tours of historic buildings in Ireland and abroad, in which friends and potential supporters were 'whirled in carriages and hearses – and occasionally motor cars – up rutted rhododendron-choked drives to surprise dozing gentry and startle nuns in the search for tumbling Palladio, obelisks, dairies and grottoes, Chinese bridges and flinty bone houses'.[7]

Desmond was urbane, Mariga was unflappable. After Princess Margaret and Lord Snowdon came to lunch at Leixlip one day in January 1965 (the couple attracted the admiring attention of a host of celebrities from the royals to Mick Jagger and Peter Sellers) two members of the IRA rang the bell and, according to Mariga, 'made some rather rude and longwinded speech about Occupied Ireland. We listened politely.'[8] The next day the men appeared on the doorstep again. They had come to apologise.

Roland Pym remembered once being driven to a dance with Mariga and an unnamed young man, who slept most of the way before waking up and being sick over his fellow-passengers. Everyone got out, appalled, and tried ineffectually to clean themselves up. Except Mariga, who stripped off her green spangled dress, threw it over a hedge, and made herself another out of leaves and branches. When they arrived at the dance, no one batted an eye.

When they bought Castletown House, the Guinnesses let it be known that they intended to open it to the public as a stately home, incorporating what Desmond described as 'a Georgian museum'. Within days, they had martialled a small army of volunteers to help with spring cleaning and painting the house. People came from neighbouring towns and villages, from Dublin, from the Trinity College Archaeological Society. Friends who came to Leixlip for the weekend found themselves taken over to Castletown where they were set to work polishing brass bannisters which were black with age. Furniture was begged or borrowed. Some of it was bought by the Guinnesses from Lord Carew. 'We are now the best-housed amenity group in the world,' Desmond declared, as he welcomed hundreds of members of the Irish Georgian Society to the re-opening of the house on Saturday 1 July 1967.[9] Their ranks were swelled that day by curious race-goers who called in on their way back from the Curragh. On three afternoons a week – Wednesday, Saturday and Sunday – visitors could pay their five shillings (one shilling for children) to wander through state rooms which, if still rather sparsely furnished, were at least being brought back to life again. 'Soon it is hoped there will be afternoon tea,' said one reporter, rather wistfully.[10]

More than 9,000 visitors came that first summer. They included Jacqueline Kennedy. The president's widow was shown round by

Desmond and Mariga one Sunday afternoon, a couple of weeks after the grand re-opening. It was a Sunday and the house was open to the public, most of whom kept a respectful distance. 'Very few tried to approach Mrs Kennedy for autographs,' reported the *Irish Independent*.[11]

The rescue of Castletown was a remarkable achievement. The Guinnesses never intended to live in the house – like the 1st Earl of Iveagh's purchase of Kenwood, it was always going to be a showcase for others to enjoy, and not a home. In 1979 the ownership of Castletown passed to a charitable trust, the Castletown Foundation, a donation on a par with Kenwood.

Let this story end with a beginning: the beginning of the conservation movement in Ireland, which owed more than words can say to two people – Desmond and Mariga Guinness.

At an IGS conference on the future of the country house in 1993, the Taoiseach, Albert Reynolds declared that such houses were now recognised as 'jewels that belong to an independent, democratic Irish nation ... we need have no complexes about their origins.'[12] That echoes a comment made nearly three centuries earlier by the Irish politician Sir John Perceval. Told of Speaker Conolly's new building project he wrote, 'I am glad for the honour of my country, that Mr Conolly has undertaken so magnificent a pile of building.'[13]

Desmond and Mariga Guinness restored that honour.

Above
Desmond Guinness with Jacqueline Kennedy at Castletown, shortly after the house was opened to the public in 1967.

Opposite
Castletown: the dining room.

Overleaf
Castletown, saved for the nation by Desmond and Mariga Guinness.

WHAT HAPPENED NEXT?

Opposite
Wilbury House, Wiltshire, the home of Rory Guinness, brother to the 4th Earl of Iveagh.

Most of the houses mentioned in this book had passed out of the Guinness family by the end of the twentieth century. Pyrford Court, the Surrey country house built by Rupert Guinness, 2nd Earl of Iveagh and his wife Gwendolen, was sold in the 1970s; after a spell as an old people's home (and a guest appearance in the 1975 horror film *The Omen*), it reverted to being a private residence. Rupert's brother Ernest's lovely Arts and Crafts mansion north of Dublin, Glenmaroon, became a convent school and is standing vacant at the time of writing. Their younger brother Walter's eccentric antiquarian concoction, Bailiffscourt, is a luxury hotel. The 1st Earl's palatial London town house at Grosvenor Place has gone.

Only here and there does life in the country house continue. In 1996, for example, the 3rd Earl of Iveagh's widow, Miranda, bought the remarkable early Palladian Wilbury House in Wiltshire, designed and built in 1710 by William Benson, who briefly replaced Sir Christopher Wren as surveyor-general of the king's works eight years later. It now belongs to her son Rory Guinness, brother to the 4th and current Earl.

Of the thirteen houses that are given chapters of their own in the preceding pages, only four remain in family hands.

Beaumont House

The Guinness family left Beaumont House, the first of their country houses, soon after the death of Arthur II in 1855, with St Anne's becoming their main country residence. In 1900 Beaumont was bought by the Sisters of Mercy, who converted it into a convalescent home, added a chapel and extended the accommodation. In spite of these changes the original five-bay house remains recognisable. It now stands within the grounds of Beaumont Hospital, one of Ireland's most important teaching hospitals.

By 2019 An Taisce, the National Trust for Ireland, designated Beaumont House as vacant and at risk. It should not be confused with the nearby public house of the same name, which is occasionally described on the internet (although not by the pub's owners, to be fair) as 'the ancestral home of Arthur Guinness'.

St Anne's

At Olive, Lady Ardilaun's death in 1925 St Anne's was left to her nephew, the Protestant clergyman Benjamin Plunket, who resigned as Bishop of Meath that year. Olive's prediction that the palatial mansion would prove too great a burden turned out to be true; and although Bishop Plunket and his family moved into St Anne's, from 1932 onwards he made several attempts to sell the house and estate. At the end of 1936 the Dublin Corporation, anxious to acquire land for housing, made an offer. But there was a considerable difference between the price Plunket asked and the official valuation, and in 1939 the Corporation decided on a Compulsory Purchase Order. That year Plunket put up the entire contents of St Anne's for auction. Widowed in 1936, and with his children grown, he moved into Sybil Hill, which was exempted from the CPO. He died in 1947, and three years later Sybil Hill was sold to the Vincentian Fathers, who used it as a school.

The main house was not so lucky. On Christmas Eve 1943 a fire broke out at St Anne's, which was being used to store air raid precaution material including gas masks and decontamination chemicals. It smouldered for three days, causing extensive damage, and for the next twenty-five years St Anne's stood as a roofless derelict shell before finally being demolished in July 1968.

Ashford Castle

St Anne's was not the only Guinness house to leave the family in 1939. That year the Iveagh trustees sold 22,000 acres of the Ashford Castle estate to the Irish state, with just over half being divided up by the Land Commission and sold to tenant farmers, and the rest cared for by the Irish Forestry Service. The contents of the house and farm buildings were sold over a two-week period that May: there were two catalogues, one

Opposite
Ashford Castle, now a luxury hotel.

describing the contents of the mansion and estate equipment, and the other listing pedigree livestock. Bidders included Lord Oranmore and Browne, husband of Ernest Guinness's daughter Oonagh. Bidding was surprisingly erratic. A dinner gong went for £7, while a bed occupied by George V on his 1905 visit went for £5 5s. 'There is no accounting for the vagaries of the buyers at the Ashford Castle auction,' remarked *The Irish Press*.[1]

The highest price on the first day's sale was £70 for the fitted dining-room carpet: it was sold to a County Kerry hotelier, Noel Huggard, who leased the castle and around 100 acres from the government and opened Ashford as a luxury sporting hotel that summer. The castle has continued to operate as a hotel under different owners since then. In 1970 it was restored and dramatically extended, doubling its size. Now offering eighty-three rooms and suites, it is currently operated by Red Carnation Hotels.

Farmleigh

The Guinness family continued to make use of Farmleigh after the 1st Earl of Iveagh's death. His eldest son Rupert, the 2nd Earl, stayed in Farmleigh when he came to Dublin. His own son Arthur was killed in 1945 and Rupert's grandson Benjamin inherited the title as 3rd Earl of Iveagh.

Left
Barack Obama and Taoiseach Enda Kenny at Farmleigh in 2011.

He and his wife Miranda, whom he married in 1963, made Farmleigh their home and in a move which was well ahead of its time, Miranda restored much of the house to the way it had been in its Edwardian heyday. At the same time Benjamin amassed an important collection of books and manuscripts covering some 800 years of Irish history, from a thirteenth-century manuscript of Gerald of Wales's *History and Topography of Ireland* to first editions of James Joyce and Seamus Heaney. The collection was donated to Marsh's Library in Dublin by the 3rd Earl's children, and remains at Farmleigh, where it is cared for by the Irish Office of Public Works.

In 1999, seven years after the 3rd Earl's death, the Guinness family decided to put Farmleigh on the market. One of only four houses in Phoenix Park, where neighbours included the President of Ireland, the American ambassador and the papal nuncio, it was bought by the Irish government as an official guesthouse for visiting foreign dignitaries. Now managed by the Office of Public Works, its state rooms have been beautifully conserved and restored, and it is open to the public.

80 St Stephen's Green

Like his father Edward Cecil, Rupert Guinness, the 2nd Earl of Iveagh, spent most of his time in England, and although he and his family made occasional use of the town house on Stephen's Green, in 1939 Rupert decided to offer it to the Irish state. It was formally accepted by the Taoiseach, Eamon de Valera, on 19 May 1939.

Renamed Iveagh House, it was generally expected that the mansion would be handed over to the National University of Ireland, the NUI, since there were university buildings next door. But in fact, it became the home of the Department of External Affairs, later the Department of Foreign Affairs, and it remains the headquarters of the DFA today.

There was already an Iveagh House in Dublin – a hostel paid for by the 1st Earl of Iveagh and opened in 1905, where 500 struggling single men could find refuge in sleeping cubicles at a rent of 3s 6d a week. ('An extra penny entitles the lodgers to a bath, with soap and towel.')[2] There is a story, probably apocryphal but too good to ignore, that visiting dignitaries hailing cabs to take them to Iveagh House for some civic function at the Department of External Affairs would sometimes be surprised to find themselves deposited at the door of the working-men's hostel instead.

Elveden Hall

The 2nd Earl of Iveagh and his wife Lady Gwendolen had no particular interest in Elveden Hall, regarding the enormous house as something of an anachronism in the mid-twentieth century. They referred to it as 'the mausoleum' and made use instead of a five-bedroomed cottage in the grounds when they stayed in Suffolk. In any case, they preferred their Surrey country house, Pyrford Court, where Lady Gwendolen laid out an important series of gardens which were heavily influenced by the ideas of Gertrude Jekyll. In the late 1940s the Pyrford head gardener still had a team of eighteen gardeners at his command.

During the First World War parts of the Elveden estate were used by the War Ministry to test the first tanks, and during the Second World War, the US Air Force's Third Air Division was headquartered at the house. The 2nd Earl, a keen agriculturalist, focused his attention on the estate. He wanted to try his hand at dairy farming, something he was already doing with a herd of Guernseys at Pyrford. He transformed the Elveden estate, reclaiming thousands of acres, subduing the rabbit population and introducing new and often experimental drainage techniques, until by the 1950s Elveden was one of the largest dairy farms in England, with an annual output of half a million gallons of milk.

The farming enterprise continues to thrive at Elveden. The house remains closed.

Kenwood

Kenwood House and the Iveagh Bequest of sixty-three paintings remain freely on view to the public, as the 1st Earl of Iveagh intended. After the Second World War, when Kenwood was taken over by the RAF Intelligence School, care of the house and collection was handed over to the London County Council, later the Greater London Council. When the GLC was abolished in 1986 responsibility for the estate was taken over by English Heritage, which has redecorated and restored several of the interiors as well as adding to the collections.

Biddesden House

As Lord and Lady Moyne, Bryan Guinness and his second wife Elisabeth lived the rest of their long lives at Biddesden where, as Lady Moyne's *Telegraph* obituary noted, 'the atmosphere was notably informal; there were seldom fewer than ten people for lunch, often more than twenty.'[3] He died in 1992, and she in 1999. The house still belongs to the family and is not open to the public.

Luttrellstown Castle

Aileen Plunket left Luttrellstown Castle in 1983. Its new owner was Didier Primat, a French billionaire. The castle was redecorated and furnished for Primat's personal use, but it soon became obvious that he intended to use it only as a holiday home, and an estate where he could indulge

Below
Comfort and splendour in the library at Luttrellstown Castle.

his interest in breeding Limousin cattle, which were introduced into the parkland in the 1980s. The house itself became a venue for society events and a sanctuary for celebrities. In 1999 it hosted the wedding of David Beckham and Spice Girl Victoria Adams, an occasion at which they were famously provided with twin golden thrones.

Plans in the early 2000s to develop the estate with the addition of an hotel, a housing estate and a second golf course (the first had been laid out in the 1980s) came to nothing; and in 2006 Luttrellstown was bought by the businessmen J.P. McManus, John Magnier and Aidan Brooks. As Luttrellstown Castle Resort it is available exclusively for private hire.

Clandeboye House

Having handed over Clandeboye in 1968 to her son Sheridan and his wife Lindy – the Marquess and Marchioness of Dufferin and Ava – Maureen Dufferin moved to England, where she lived in the sixteenth-century Owl House at Lamberhurst in Kent. In later life (she died in 1998 at the age of ninety-one) she became embroiled in a series of unfortunate legal disputes. In one case she was taken to an industrial tribunal in England by her estate manager and housekeeper, a married couple. They successfully claimed unfair dismissal after Maureen accused them of, among other things, stealing fruit from her favourite crab apple tree. And fourteen years later her daughters Caroline and Perdita and her daughter-in-law Lindy took Lady Dufferin to court to overturn her plan to make her two granddaughters the beneficiaries of a £15 million trust fund in their place. This time she won.

Below
Lindy Guinness, the Marchioness of Dufferin and Ava, painting at Clandeboye.

In the meantime Sheridan and Lindy made a number of changes to Clandeboye. They moved the kitchen from a distant wing, placing it next door to the dining room – 'to lessen the domestic burden,' said Lindy, noting that the couple now had a domestic staff of four people, 'magicians [who] do the work of a staff that once was twenty.'[4] An accomplished artist who called Bloomsburyite Duncan Grant her teacher and mentor, Lindy turned the old kitchen into her studio, and she and her husband, a great patron of the arts, both added furniture, paintings and sculpture to the various state rooms.

Sheridan died of AIDS in 1988, aged 49. Lindy, who survived him for another thirty-two years, wrote that Clandeboye was 'a house of dreams and enchantment that fill my thoughts and, as I grow older, the pleasure of being part of it grows greater.'[5]

The house is not open to the public.

Luggala

In later life Oonagh Oranmore and Browne made her home in Guernsey, although she returned to Ireland in 1993. She died at Luggala in August 1995. Garech Browne, the surviving son from her marriage to Dominick, the 4th Lord Oranmore and Browne, inherited the house and continued his mother's tradition of entertaining on a magnificent and chaotic scale. He was also a discerning patron of the arts, championing the cause of Irish traditional music – he began his own record label, Claddagh Records, in 1959, and the Chieftains were among early signings – and counting artists of the stature of Francis Bacon and Lucian Freud among his friends. Browne enjoyed the company of actors and poets and singers: visitors to Luggala included Dennis Hopper, Marianne Faithfull, Mick and Bianca Jagger, Ronnie Wood and Seamus Heaney.

Shortly before his death in 2018, Garech Browne put Luggala and its 5000-acre estate on the market. There was talk at the time of it being bought by the Irish government, but the price tag of €28 million proved a little too much, and Luggala went to a private buyer. It is not open to the public.

Kelvedon Hall

In spite of describing Kelvedon as Heartbreak House after his wife Honor Guinness left him, 'Chips' Channon held on to the hall. One of the last entries in his diary, before a series of strokes incapacitated him, was

GUINNESS

Opposite
Detail of the mural in Honor Channon's bathroom at Kelvedon, with a bottle of Guinness added in the recent restoration by Ashe Ericksson.

Below
Desmond Guinness at the unveiling of Arthur Guinness Square in Leixlip in 2012.

Overleaf
The Doric bath house at Luttrellstown Castle, seen from across the lake.

'Lovely blue day. Kelvedon at its best.'[6] He died in October 1958 and was buried by the ruined chapel in the grounds of the house.

As Lady Honor Svejdar, Chips's ex-wife moved to Ireland, where she became a successful breeder of racehorses. She also had a house on the fashionable island of Mustique in the Grenadines. She died in 1976.

Kelvedon Hall remains in the Channon family. It is open to the public by appointment.

Castletown House

Desmond and Mariga Guinness's work in rescuing Castletown House was continued by the Castletown Foundation, which was established in 1979 to own, maintain and restore this, one of the most important of all Irish country houses. An acrimonious divorce in 1983 saw Mariga evicted from Leixlip (although she later returned to live there) and Desmond having to find £500,000 by way of a settlement. He was forced to sell furniture and paintings which the Foundation was able to buy for Castletown House.

By the early 1990s the Foundation's trustees realised that conservation was urgently needed, on a scale that was far beyond their means; and in 1994 the house was taken over by the Irish government, who tasked the Office of Public Works with managing the work. The OPW carried out a major structural programme in the later 1990s and began the slow process of reclaiming parts of the wider estate. To date around 227 acres of the historic grounds are in public ownership.

At the time of writing, Castletown House is closed to the public, the result of a long-running and increasingly bitter battle with local residents over rights of way and vehicular access. When good sense eventually prevails, as it surely must, the house will once again open its doors to visitors who come to marvel at Desmond Guinness's great legacy.

Notes

1. Beaumont House

1 Lynch and Vaizey 1960, p. 8.
2 Lynch and Vaizey 1960, p. 104.
3 Lynch and Vaizey 1960, p. 106.
4 Guinness 1999, p. 73.
5 Lynch and Vaizey 1960, p. 108.
6 Guinness 1999, p. 73.
7 *Farmer's Gazette and Journal of Practical Horticulture*, 20 December 1851, p. 10.
8 Lynch and Vaizey 1960, p. 108.
9 *Saunders's News-Letter*, 11 June 1855, p. 3.

2. St Anne's

1 Guinness 1999, pp. 70–2.
2 Guinness 1999, p. 72.
3 Guinness 1999, p. 75.
4 *John Bull*, 24 April 1880, 264.
5 Fuller 1920, p. 215.
6 *Tatler*, 8 February 1905, p. 212.
7 *Queen*, 6 September 1902, p. 364.
8 Robinson 1947, p. 222.
9 Everett 1951, p. 157.
10 Everett 1951, p. 159.
11 Everett 1951, p. 162.
12 Everett 1951, p. 162.
13 Everett 1951, p. 173.
14 Will of Olivia Lady Ardilaun, 1926: CS/HC/PO/4/79/69, National Archives of Ireland.
15 *The Times*, 15 March 1926, p. 16.

3. Ashford Castle

1 Burke 1858, p. 242; quoted in Wilde 1867, p. 184.
2 https://www.buildingsofireland.ie/buildings-search/building/30402719/ashford-castle-ashford-or-cappacorcorcoge-conga-cong-co-galway [accessed 5 August 2025].
3 Wilde, 1867, p. 183. Wilde is quoting (and agreeing with) Sir Bernard Burke.
4 *Freeman's Journal*, 29 August 1871, p. 6.
5 Moore 1887, p. 183.
6 Clesham 2015, pp. 155–70, p. 168.
7 Clesham 2015, 155–70, p. 168.
8 Moore 1887, pp. 67–8.
9 Moore 1887, p. 69.
10 Moore 1887, p. 67.
11 *Drogheda Conservative*, 13 July 1872, p. 3.
12 *Daily Telegraph*, 25 January 1905, p. 10.
13 Black 1906, p. 237.

4. Farmleigh

1 https://sirwilliamorpen.com/edward-cecil-guinness-1st-earl-of-iveagh-by-sir-william-orpen-at-farmleigh/[accessed 25 August 2025].
2 Martelli 1956, p. 61.
3 https://www.masseysagency.co.uk/[accessed 25 August 2025].
4 https://www.gracesguide.co.uk/Morison_and_Co [accessed 25 August 2025].
5 *Daily Telegraph*, 18 April 1900, p. 8.
6 *Daily Telegraph*, 18 April 1900, p. 8.
7 *Daily Telegraph*, 19 April 1900, p. 7.
8 *Daily Telegraph*, 19 April 1900, p. 7.
9 *Mackenzie & Moncur Ltd., Hothouse Builders, Heating and Ventilating Engineers*, Abridged [sic] Catalogue (1901).

Interlude: The Houses of God

1 https://www.dia.ie/architects/view/3759/MCCARTHY-JAMESJOSEPH#tab_biography [accessed 25 August 2025].

Opposite
Rococo plasterwork in the staircase hall at Castletown.

2 *Dublin Builder*, 15 January 1863, pp. 4–5.
3 *Daily Telegraph*, 20 April 1868, p. 3.
4 *Ecclesiologist* 23 (1862), p. 340.
5 *Ecclesiologist* 25 (1864), pp. 173, 213, 220.
6 *Freeman's Journal*, 27 January 1863, p. 3.
7 *Dublin Builder*, 1 April 1863, p. 57.

5. 80 St Stephen's Green

1 Cork and Orrery 1903, I, p. 206.
2 https://www.dib.ie/biography/castle-castles-cassels-cassells-richard-a1552 [accessed 25 August 2025].
3 Cork and Orrery, 1903, I, p. 177.
4 *Tatler*, 22 October 1902, p. 21.
5 Fingall and Hinkson 1991, p. 303.
6 Fingall and Hinkson 1991, p. 288.
7 Fingall and Hinkson 1991, p. 288.
8 *Henley Advertiser*, 14 August 1897, p. 2.
9 The *Whitehall Review*, quoted in Gerard 1898, p. 403.
10 *Freeman's Journal*, 1 July 1887, p. 5.
11 *Evening Herald*, 18 July 1899, p. 2.

6. Elveden Hall

1 Martelli 1956, p. 199.
2 *York Herald*, 21 November 1889, p. 6.
3 Martelli 1956, p. 204
4 Earl of Cardigan, 'The Wardens of Savernake Forest Part IV: The Brudenell Wardens,' *The Wiltshire Magazine*, 53 (1949), p. 44.
5 Hare 1896–1900, p. 6, p. 400.
6 Hare 1896–1900, p. 6, p. 400.
7 Martelli 1956, p. 213.
8 Clive Aslet, 'Elveden Hall, Suffolk – II,' *Country Life*, 15 March 1984, p. 674.
9 Swinton Jacob 1890, p. 1, preface.
10 Quoted in Clive Aslet, 'Elveden Hall, Suffolk – II,' *Country Life*, 15 March 1984, p. 674.
11 Clive Aslet, 'Elveden Hall, Suffolk – II,' *Country Life*, 15 March 1984, p. 672.
12 Fingall and Hinkson, p. 337.
13 Clive Aslet, 'Elveden Hall, Suffolk – II,' *Country Life*, 15 March 1984, p. 672.
14 *Tatler*, 29 November 1905, p. 20.
15 Martelli 1956, p. 206.
16 *Bristol Times and Mirror*, 12 December 1903, p. 3.
17 Fingall and Hinkson 1991, p. 296.
18 Fingall and Hinkson 1991, pp. 305–6.

7. Kenwood House

1 Martelli 1956, p. 292.
2 *Sunday Express*, 24 September 1922, p. 14.
3 *The Times*, 6 December 1924, p. 13.
4 *Country Life*, 28 March 1925, p. 467.
5 Martelli 1956, pp. 86–7, quoting Behrman's biography of Joseph Duveen.
6 Martelli 1956, p. 143.
7 Martelli 1956, p. 87.
8 Martelli 1956, p. 144.
9 *The Times*, 8 October 1927, p. 6.
10 *Belfast Newsletter*, 8 October 1927, p. 6.
11 *Irish Independent*, 8 October 1927, p. 6.
12 https://www.legislation.gov.uk/ukla/Geo5/19-20/69/pdfs/ukla_19290069_en.pdf [accessed 25 August 2025].
13 Iveagh Bequest Act 1929, schedule, clause 6(c).
14 Iveagh Bequest Act 1929, schedule, clause 7(c).
15 *Daily Herald*, 19 July 1928, p. 5.

8. Biddesden House

1 https://historicengland.org.uk/listing/the-list/list-entry/1027676?section=official-list-entry [accessed 25 August 2025].
2 *Liverpool Daily Post*, 31 July 1931, p. 6.
3 Guinness 1982, p. 45.
4 Guinness 1982, p. 48.
5 Christopher Hussey, 'Biddesden House – I,' *Country Life*, 2 April 1938, p. 356.
6 Betjeman 1994–5, I, p. 98.
7 Mosley 2002, p. 82.
8 Mosley 2002, p. 82.
9 *The Times*, 16 June 1933, p. 4.

9. Luttrellstown Castle

1 *Sunday Independent*, 26 June 1983, p. 2.
2 *Sunday Telegraph*, 18 September 1983, p. 48.
3 *Kerry Reporter*, 21 May 1932, p. 5.
4 Heffer 2021, p. 675.
5 106 *Irish Independent*, 9 February 1940, p. 4.
6 *Yorkshire Post and Leeds Intelligencer*, 21 May 1945, p. 2.
7 *Daily Express*, 8 January 1960, p. 3.
8 *Nottingham Guardian*, 13 June 1972, p. 9.
9 *Sunday Express*, 12 November 1972, p. 3.
10 *Sunday Telegraph*, 18 September 1983, p. 9.
11 *Sunday Independent*, 26 June 1983, p. 2.
12 *The Times*, 29 September 1983, p. 4.

10. Clandeboye House

1 Stamp 1985, p. 28.
2 Stamp 1985, p. 33.
3 Nicolson 1937, p. 51.
4 Nicolson 1937, p. 138.
5 Betjeman 1994–5, I, p. 77.
6 Nicolson 1937, pp. 95–6.
7 *Market Harborough Advertiser and Midland Mail*, 28 August 1931, p. 3.
8 Nicolson 1937, p. 76.
9 *Tatler*, 21 September 1932, p. 493.
10 *Tatler*, 9 October 1935, p. 83.
11 *Tatler*, 3 August 1938, p. 207.
12 *Belfast Newsletter*, 17 November 1941, p. 3.
13 Heffer 2022, p. 256.
14 Betjeman 1945, pp. 120–1.
15 *Tatler*, 30 July 1952, p. 190.

11. Kelvedon Hall

1 Christopher Hussey, '5 Belgrave Square, London: The Residence of Mr Henry and Lady Honor Channon,' *Country Life*, 26 February 1938, p. 224.
2 Nicolson 1966, p. 244.
3 Heffer 2021, p. 449.
4 Christopher Hussey, 'Kelvedon Hall, Essex – II,' *Country Life*, 10 May 1941, p. 410.
5 Heffer 2021, p. 699.
6 Heffer 2021, p. 917.
7 Heffer 2021, p. 887.
8 Heffer 2021, p. 891.
9 *Daily News*, 6 July 1934, p. 5.
10 *Bystander*, 20 March 1935, p. 492.
11 Heffer 2021, p. 34.
12 Heffer 2021, p. 398.
13 Heffer 2021, p. 216.
14 Evelyn Waugh to Randolph Churchill, 26 September 1941, in Amory 1980, p. 154.
15 Heffer 2021, p. 529.
16 Heffer 2021, p. 529.

12. Luggala

1 O'Byrne 2012, p. 44.
2 Fielding 1954, p. 113.
3 *Tatler*, 25 March 1931, p. 53.
4 Quoted in O'Byrne 2012, p. 104.
5 https://www.independent.co.uk/news/obituaries/obituary-oonagh-oranmore-1595833.html [accessed 25 August 2025].
6 Viertel 1992, p. 288.
7 Partridge 1985, 164.
8 *Irish Press*, 22 November, 1963, p. 2.
9 Partridge 1985, p. 165.
10 *Tatler*, 3 February 1960, p. 30.
11 *Tatler*, 3 February 1960, p. 30.
12 *Evening Herald*, 29 June 1960, p. 5.
13 *Irish Examiner*, 14 September 1964, p. 1.
14 Frederic Mullally, *The Silver Salver: The Story of the Guinness Family* (Granada, 1981), p. 150.
15 *Belfast Newsletter*, 15 July 1965, p. 3.
16 *Sunday Telegraph*, 13 March 1966, p. 27.
17 *Daily Express*, 25 April 1966, p. 3.
18 Howard 2017, p. 247.
19 *Ireland's Saturday Night*, 23 April 1966, p. 7.
20 Howard 2017, p. 5.

13. Castletown House

1 *Country Life*, 25 March 1965, Supplement, p. 17.
2 Loveday 1890, p. 48.
3 https://www.rte.ie/archives/2020/0401/1127802-castletown-house-sold/ [accessed 25 August 2025].
4 https://src.apollo-magazine.com/an-amplitude-of-personal-charm-desmond-guinness-1931-2020/ [accessed 25 August 2025].
5 https://www.irishtimes.com/culture/art-and-design/1950s-dublin-saving-grand-old-houses-from-the-politicians-who-hated-them-1.3409327 [accessed 25 August 2025].
6 *Country Life*, 19 July 2001, p. 102.
7 *Daily Telegraph*, 10 May 1989, p. 21.
8 Peck 1997, p. 126.
9 *Nationalist and Leinster Times*, 7 July 1967, p. 41.
10 *Nenagh Guardian*, 15 July 1967, p. 3.
11 *Irish Independent*, 17 July 1967, p. 1.
12 *Country Life*, 28 May 1998, p. 89.
13 Bland 1914, pp. 194–5.

What Happened Next?

1 *Irish Press*, 18 May 1939, p. 8.
2 *Irish Independent*, 19 July 1905, p. 6.
3 *Daily Telegraph*, 28 January 1999, p. 31.
4 *Clandeboye*, pp. 12–13.
5 *Clandeboye*, p. 16.
6 Heffer 2022, p. 1091.

Bibliography

Amory 1980

Mark Amory, ed., *The Letters of Evelyn Waugh.* London, 1980.

Bence-Jones 1998

Mark Bence-Jones, *A Guide to Irish Country Houses*. London, 1998.

Betjeman 1945

John Betjeman, 'In Memory of Basil, Marquess of Dufferin and Ava,' verse 3, line 8, in *New Bats in Old Belfries.* London, 1945.

Betjeman 1994–5

John Betjeman, *Letters*, 2 vols. London, 1994–5.

Black 1906

Adam and Charles Black (publisher), *Black's Guide to Ireland*, 24th edition. London, 1906.

Bland 1914

Benjamin Bland, ed., *Berkeley and Percival: The Correspondence of George Berkeley, afterwards Bishop of Cloyne, and Sir John Percival, afterwards Earl of Egmont.* Cambridge, 1914.

Bryant 1990

Julius Bryant, *The Iveagh Bequest: Kenwood*. London, 1990.

Casey 2005

Christine Casey, *The Buildings of Ireland: Dublin.* New Haven and London, 2005.

Clandeboye 1985

Lady Dufferin, 'Clandeboye in my Life,' *Clandeboye.* Antrim, 1985.

Clesham 2015

Brigid Clesham, 'Gertrude Clements' Journal of a Visit to the Maam Valley in 1880,' *Journal of the Galway Archaeological and Historical Society*. Galway, 2015.

Cork and Orrery 1903

Countess of Cork and Orrery, ed., *The Orrery Papers*, 2 vols. London, 1903.

Dennison and MacDonagh 1998

S.R. Dennison and Oliver MacDonagh, *Guinness 1886–1939: From Incorporation to the Second World War*. Cork, 1998.

Dooley 2001
Terence Dooley, *The Decline of the Big House in Ireland: a Study of Irish Landed Families, 1860–1960*. Dublin, 2001.
Dooley 2022
Terence Dooley, *Burning the Big House: The Story of the Irish Country House in a Time of War and Revolution*. New Haven and London, 2022.
Everett 1951
Katherine Everett, *Bricks and Flowers*. London, 1951.
Fielding 1954
Daphne Fielding, *Mercury Presides*. London, 1954.
Fingall and Hinkson 1991
Elizabeth, Countess of Fingall, and Pamela Hinkson, *Seventy Years Young*. Dublin, 1991.
Fuller 1920
J.F. Fuller, *Omniana: The Autobiography of an Irish Octogenarian, New and Enlarged Edition*. London, 1920.
Gerard 1898
Frances Gerard, *Picturesque Dublin Old and New*. London, 1898.
Guinness 1982
Bryan Guinness, *Pot-pourri From the Thirties*. Burford, 1982.
Guinness 1997
Jonathan Guinness, *Requiem for a Family Business*. London, 1997.
Guinness 1999
Michele Guinness, *The Guinness Spirit: Brewers and Bankers, Ministers and Missionaries*. London, 1999.
Guinness 2008
Patrick Guinness, *Arthur's Round: The Life and Times of Brewing Legend Arthur Guinness*. London, 2008.
Hare 1896–1900
Augustus Hare, *The Story of My Life*, 6 vols. London, 1896–1900.
Heffer 2021
Simon Heffer, ed., *Henry 'Chips' Channon, The Diaries: 1938–43*. London, 2021.
Heffer 2022
Simon Heffer, ed., *Henry 'Chips' Channon, The Diaries: 1943–57*. London, 2022.

Hill, undated
Judith Hill, *Farmleigh*. Dublin, n.d.
Houliston and Jenkins 2014
Laura Houliston and Susan Jenkins, *Kenwood: The Iveagh Bequest*. London, 2014.
Howard 2017
Paul Howard, *I Read the News Today, Oh Boy*. London, 2017.
Jacob 1890
Colonel Samuel Swinton Jacob, *Jeypore Portfolio of Architectural Details*, 6 vols. London, 1890.
Lees-Milne 1984
James Lees-Milne, *Prophesying Peace*. London, 1984.
Loveday 1890
John Edward Taylor Loveday, ed., *Diary of a Tour in 1732 Through Parts of England, Wales, Ireland and Scotland, made by John Loveday of Caversham*. Edinburgh, 1890.
Lowell 2010
Ivana Lowell, *Why Not Say What Happened? A Memoir*. London, 2010.
Lynch and Vaizey 1960
Patrick Lynch and John Vaizey, *Guinness's Brewery in the Irish Economy 1759–1876*. Cambridge, 1960.
Martelli 1956
George Martelli, *Man of His Time: A Life of the First Earl of Iveagh K.P., G.C.V.O.* London, 1956.
Moore 1887
George Moore, *Parnell and His Island*. London, 1887.
Mosley 1985
Diana Mosley, *A Life of Contrasts*. London, 2002.
Mulally 1981
Frederic Mullally, *The Silver Salver: The Story of the Guinness Family*. London, 1981.
Nicolson 1937
Harold Nicolson, *Helen's Tower*. London, 1937.
Nicolson 1966
Nigel Nicolson, ed., *Harold Nicolson, Diaries and Letters 1930–1939*. London, 1966.

O'Byrne 2012
Robert O'Byrne, *Luggala Days: The Story of a Guinness House.* London, 2012.
Partridge 1985
Frances Partridge, *Everything To Lose: Diaries 1945–1960.* London, 1985.
Peck 1997
Carola Peck, *Mariga and her Friends.* Ballivor, 1997.
Robinson 1947
Lennox Robinson, ed., *Lady Gregory's Journals 1916–1930.* London, 1947.
Schoenberger 2001
Nancy Schoenberger, *Dangerous Muse: The Life of Lady Caroline Blackwood.* London, 2001.
Sharkey 2002
Joan Ussher Sharkey, *St Anne's: The Story of a Guinness Estate.* Dublin, 2002.
Sheaff 1978
Nicholas Sheaff, *Iveagh House: An Historical Description.* Dublin, 1978.
Stamp 1985
Gavin Stamp, 'Helen's Tower', *Clandeboye.* Belfast, 1985.
Tinniswood 2021
Adrian Tinniswood, *Noble Ambitions: The Fall and Rise of the Post-War Country House.* London, 2021.
Tinniswood 2024
Adrian Tinniswood, *The Power and the Glory: The Country House Before the Great War.* London, 2024.
Viertel 1992
Peter Viertel, *Dangerous Friends: At Large With Huston and Hemingway in the Fifties.* London, 1992.
Walsh 2007
Patrick Walsh, *Castletown, Co. Kildare.* Dublin, 2007.
Wilde 1867
Sir William Wilde, *Lough Corrib, Its Shores and Islands.* Dublin, 1867.
Wilson 1998
Derek Wilson, *Dark and Light: The Story of the Guinness Family.* London, 1998.

Acknowledgements

Many people have helped me with the writing of this book, offering introductions and information, practical guidance and moral support. I particularly want to thank the Earl of Iveagh; Katie Channon; Rosaleen Mulji; Polly Powell at Batsford Books, who first came to me with the idea for a book on the Guinness family's houses; John Stachiewicz, whose chairmanship of Batsford provided me with an opportunity to renew an old and valued friendship; Claire Young, Oliver Craske and the team at Scala; my excellent editor Rachel Giles; the book's designer, James Alexander. Niall Rochford and his staff, who welcomed me so warmly to Ashford Castle; the lovely team at Luttrellstown Castle; Aisling from the Office of Public Works, who gave me such a fabulous and informative tour of Farmleigh; Professor Terence Dooley of the Centre for the Study of Historic Irish Houses and Estates at Maynooth University, whose help and encouragement have meant a lot to me; Robert O'Byrne, whose writings on Irish houses continue to be an inspiration; contributors to the Country Houses of the UK and Ireland Facebook group, whose combined knowledge of the subject is breathtaking; librarians at Maynooth University, the London Library and the University of Buckingham; and everyone at the Sea Rod Inn, Doohoma, who kept me sane while I was writing the book, especially Sinéad Gallagher, who poured the Guinness.

Last, first, always, my thanks to Helen, without whom nothing would be possible.

Picture Credits

Front cover: Photographer/Artist: Doug McKinlay Getty Images (UK) Limited. George Munday/Alamy: p. 1; p. 36; p. 141; pp. 218–19. Robert O'Byrne (The Irish Aesthete): p. 2; p. 30; p.31; p. 34; p. 39; p. 35; p. 54; p. 62; p. 63; p, 67; p. 126; p. 138; p. 148; p. 183; p. 185. 4H4/Alamy: pp. 4–5. © Toby Webster Photography: p. 8; p. 165; p. 168; p. 169; 170; 171; 172; pp. 173–74; p. 176; p. 216. Martyn Boyd/Alamy: p. 10. Guinness Archive, Diageo Ireland: p. 14; p. 15; p. 16; p. 18; p. 19; pp. 20–21; p. 22; p. 23; p. 28; p. 77; p. 95 (bottom). Courtesy of the National Inventory of Architectural Heritage, National Built Heritage Service, Ireland: p. 17. Bibliotheque Nationale de France: p. 19; Dawid Kalisinski/Alamy: p. 26. Courtesy of Irish Architectural Archive: p. 27. Creative commons: p. 33; p. 75 (top); p. 84; Bricks and Flowers, Katherine Everitt, 1951, The Reprint Society: p. 41. Shutterstock: pp. 42–43; p. 44; p. 57; pp. 72–73; p. 112 (both); p. 114; p. 180; p. 191. Ros Drinkwater/Alamy: p. 46; p. 47; p. 209. Penta Springs Limited/Alamy: p. 48; (bottom). Look and Learn/ Illustrated Papers Collection/ Bridgeman Images: p. 50. Hemis/Alamy: p. 53. Photo Courtesy Priory Studios: p. 56; p. 58; p. 87. Courtesy of Earl of Iveagh; p. 61 (top, middle); p. 86; p. 90; p. 97; p. 99; p. 101; p. 106 (both); 109; p. 124. © Country Life/Future Publishing Ltd; p. 61 (bottom); p. 130 (left); p. 131; p. 132; p. 133; p. 134; p. 142; p. 150; p. 155; p. 157; p. 160; p. 163; p. 166; p. 214. © Davison & Associates Ltd: p. 64, p. 65; p. 87. p. 202. Canadian Centre for Architecture: p. 70; © Mary Evans Picture Library: p. 71. Public domain: p. 92. Peter Etteridge/Alamy, p. 75. James Schwabel/Alamy, p. 76. De Luan/ Alamy: p. 79. Walter Bibikow/Alamy: p. 81. The Irish Image Collection/Alamy: p. 82. Courtesy of B. T. Batsford: p. 85. Whyte's Irish Art & Collectables Auctioneers: p. 91. © Coronet Images/Peter Bance Collection: p. 96. Oliver Craske: p. 100; p. 102. Heritage Image Partnership Ltd/Alamy: 103. Keith Mindham/Alamy: pp. 104–5. Chronicle/Alamy: p. 108; p. 128; p. 181. Arcaid Images/Alamy: p. 110. Photo12/Ann Ronan Picture Library/Alamy; p. 111. Photo Prisma Archivo/Alamy. p. 113. Ian G Dagnall/Alamy: p. 115; p. 123. John Michaels/Alamy: p. 116. © London Transport Museum; p. 117. Tony French/Alamy: p. 119. Bill Batten/Alamy: p. 118. © Simon Upton /Interior Archive: p. 125; p. 136. Chroma Collection/Alamy: p. 127. © National Portrait Gallery, London: p. 130 (right). Courtesy by Anthony Eyre: p. 137. Courtesy of Luttrellstown Resort: p. 139; p. 143; p. 144; pp. 146–47; p. 213. Photo, National Gallery of Ireland: p. 140. Smith Archive/Alamy:

p. 151; p. 156; p. 164; p. 182; p. 200. The Print Collector/Alamy: p. 150. David Murphy/Alamy: p. 153. © Illustrated London News Ltd./Mary Evans: p. 158. SuperStock/Alamy: p. 162. Artepics/Alamy: p. 178. Padi Prints/Troy TV Stock/Alamy: p. 179. Trinity Mirror/Mirrorpix /Alamy: p. 187. United Archives GmbH/Alamy: p. 189. © Film still from *Art on Wheels*, 1966. Courtesy British Pathé: 190. Image Source Limited /Alamy: p. 192. Danvis Collection/Alamy: p. 193. Eye Ubiquitous/Alamy: p. 195; p. 198; p. 199; p. 202; pp. 204–5. © Courtesy Rory Guinness: p. 206. World Politics Archive (WPA)/Alamy: p. 210. WENN Rights Ltd/Alamy: p, 217.

Index

Page numbers for illustrations are in *italics*.